Dancing in the Doghouse

Sharing God's Presence in Everyday Places

Alisa E. Clark

Dancing in the Doghouse, Age 38

2010 Full Color Edition
ISBN: 1-4392-5867-8

Photography by Paula Betts
of Alphabetts Portrait Studio
info@alphabetts.com

Edited by Cherilyn D. Johnson, MA, LLPC
Sparrow's Nest Christian Counseling
ionthesparrow@gmail.com

Additional copies can be purchased through www.journeyoncanvas.com

Acknowledgements

I can't even begin to figure out how to thank everyone. There are too many people to thank. The names of all the people who have touched my life would extend well beyond the scope of these pages. Generous family, loving friends and kind acquaintances, you have loved me well and I desire to thank you. You are part of my story and I am overwhelmingly grateful for you.

There are a few key players who must be mentioned. I would never have had the guts to go through with this project without the encouragement of my husband, Craig. I would never have had the courage to face the obstacles of the last decade without my children. Emily, AJ and Zachary, you have given my life great purpose.

Finally, thank God! I didn't do anything special to earn the honor of His appearance throughout my life. He's been there because, for some mind-boggling reason, He loves me. He's the reason why I live, breathe and take joy in the journey. He is my greatest acknowledgement.

Let It Matter

My ordinary life~
Let it not be a meaningless journey~
Where only bad is found where there is also much good~
In which happiness has been lost and forgotten~
Memories are only of pain, sadness and loss~

Instead,
Let what is good shine in the dark places~
What was right silence what is best forgotten~
May truth call into the light what heals, gives joy and brings life~
Redeem my journey, Lord.
Please.
Let it matter.

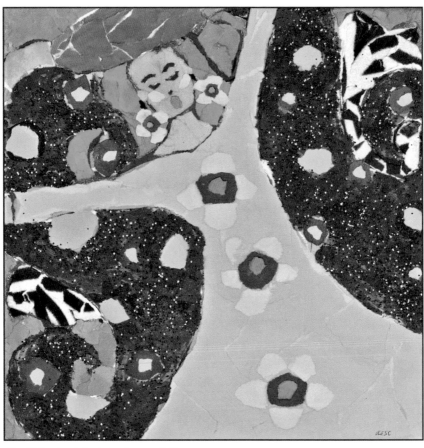

Call into Light, Age 39

Contents

Prologue

It's easy to think that we have to do something, or experience something, remarkable to have a reason to share the story of our lives. We have a way of believing that our ordinary lives are powerless. The value in reaching out is missed in our poor estimation of what we have to offer. We wait for something big to happen to us before we recognize the importance of our journey. We don't acknowledge the special gift we have to share. It's the gift of our ordinary lives shared with others.

I joined a codependency support group. The people in my group are extraordinary. They're not, however, extraordinary by a worldly definition. None of the people at the table are famous, exceedingly rich or outrageously successful. They are ordinary people living ordinary lives. I learn from their lives. They live simply, and honorably, in the face of great adversity. In fact, adversity transforms them, making them gentler, kinder and more forgiving. I admire their stamina and their confidence in God's plan for their lives. Their journeys encourage me.

For a while, I felt like I had no business taking a spot at the support group table. I expected to have very little to offer, or receive from, the people sitting around me. Then, it started to happen. As stories were shared I began to connect with people. Some days I discovered that we had the same feelings. Other days I found myself working through the same problem as someone to the left or the right of me. Our lives began to intersect. Common threads connected their journeys to mine. Their stories filled my world with hope. I began to expect that I would have something to receive.

Some days, when the meeting was over, people would thank me for having shared. My journey touched others and encouraged them. They found healing through my expression of the simple, ordinary experiences of my life. My stories filled their world with hope. I began to see that I not only had something to receive; I had something to offer.

I have a journey to share. It's not earth-shattering or surprisingly unique. It's an ordinary story about an ordinary life. It's a life that has ups and downs and in betweens just like yours. It's my hope that my journey shared will be a gift just for you. I pray that as you read about my journey you will find common threads that connect your life to mine. God willing, my journey will touch and encourage you.

Perhaps you have an ordinary life that's a little like mine? Maybe we should both share our journeys? Together we could reach out to even more people who could reach out as well. Imagine all the people who would realize that they are not alone. Imagine all the people who could be touched, encouraged and healed by the simple truth that a shared journey is a gift worth sharing.

If you do choose to tell the story of your life, I want to offer you one simple encouragement. Tell it in your own, unique way. Everyone brings their special touch to the expression of their journey, making the experience of telling and receiving stories a flavorful and powerful experience. Parts of my journey happen to have been captured on a canvas. This is just one way of giving the journey expression. I encourage you to embrace these expressions rather than be discouraged by them. It's your story. Tell it your way. Let others do the same. Enjoy the ways God has made us all unique.

I'm an artist. I'm going to share my journey as an artist would. I'd never paint on a canvas before it was stretched on a frame. In the same way, I won't try to share my journey without first giving you a framework, or a context, for what you will see and read throughout the pages of this book. There are pieces of my past that will help build that framework, so I want to introduce them. They are my reason for "Remembering."

Share
Your
Story

My Spot Awaits Me, Age 39

Remembering

Birthplace, Age 25

I was born on May 30th, 1968, in a suburb about 30 miles north of New York City. I was an average kid living in the burbs. I wasn't extraordinarily talented or gifted. Nothing remarkable happened to me or for me. Most of my early memories are of ordinary things. They were all pretty simple, ordinary memories but they spoke to me of much greater things. It's not what happened to me, but how it all drew me to God that's the fuel for my story. How I found God through each simple moment is my story to share.

I remember that I was very sheltered as a child. My childhood home was an old farmhouse surrounded by two acres of remarkable beauty. Our yard was filled with green grass, gigantic pine trees, tons of wildlife and lots of fruit to pick and eat. Our home was centered within 10 acres of forest that separated us from the outside world. It was our own little paradise. It all suggested that someone great had made it all.

I recall saying prayers before dinner. That was the only time my family made any reference to God. Recognizing and enjoying beauty was my family's religion. My dad was a scientist, so it was natural for him to investigate things. It was also natural for him to share his discoveries with us. He was often the first to notice the crocuses budding in the spring. He'd snip a few and bring them inside. He'd place them in a little glass cup with water and show them off in the middle of the kitchen table. This was just one way he drew our attention to the beauty around us. We were surrounded by incredible beauty, so Dad didn't need to look far to find something wondrous to share. What he shared with me were hints that there might be one great creator. It all begged the question, "How could the world be so fantastic if there isn't a God?"

One of my first memories is a weak recollection of being baptized in the Greek Orthodox Church. I remember being naked in front of a whole bunch of people and saying, "I don't like this bath!" I was embarrassed and upset. My baptism didn't feel special. It felt weird and scary. I knew something big was happening, though. I was given a gold chain with a cross on the end of it. I was warned to take special care of it. I recognized that the cross was the part that was really important.

I also have some faint memories of a nursery school that had a nun in an office. Sometimes, the nun was happy to see me. She'd talk to me. Other days she wasn't safe. She'd be grumpy and close the door. This man named "Jesus" hung on her wall. I didn't know who He was but I was curious about Him.

I first met Jesus when I played Mary in the first grade Christmas pageant. I was dressed in a blue and white gown. Sister Marianne put Kelly, my favorite doll, in a white cotton swaddle and placed her in my arms. I stood on the stage feeling incredibly special. I looked out at the lights, and the people in the audience, baffled at how I got to be Jesus' mom. I figured Jesus must like me to choose me to be His mom.

At Saint Augustine's elementary school I was indoctrinated into this thing called "Catholic." Being a Greek Orthodox kid,

I received communion before my Catholic classmates. I approached the front of the church to receive as all the first graders watched me. I had no idea what I was doing. The priest said, "The body of Christ," and I just looked at him. I didn't even know I was supposed to say, "Amen." All I knew for sure was that Jesus had something to do with it all.

The nuns at Saint Augustine's told me that Jesus could heal people. I can go back pretty far in my childhood and recall that I had already begun asking Him to heal me. I had trouble sleeping so I needed help. I remember being seven years old, maybe less, and already praying and asking Jesus for a good night's sleep. I recall that a good part of the time I didn't get one. I know I was really young at the time because of the music boxes. When I was little I had four of them. Three of them would be wound up at the base and one had a pull string and a Hummel on its flat face. My dad would wind up all four of them at night when he tucked me in. He'd come back, and do it again, if I was still awake when he made his rounds later in the evening. Sometimes he'd come back two or three times. The music boxes didn't fix my sleep troubles but they comforted me. They showed me that my dad understood and wanted to help. I figured that Jesus gave me a nice dad, so I would know that He cared. Dad was one of my first tastes of God's love and my first memory of an answer to prayer.

Special people had special ways of being the touch of God just for me. It's that special touch that made me a child who knew God was with her and around her. My mom is one of the special people who had The Touch. She told me that she loved me and she was the one who brought me to see I was an artist. She made me believe I had something important to make, say and share. Her tenderness and encouragement were God's voice.

Mom had The Touch. She also had a lot of up and down days. Some days she'd be full of enthusiasm for people and things we could do together. We'd hold hands, go shopping in Nyack and have lunch together at the Strawberry Place. She'd listen to me and tell me that I was her friend. She'd say I was her "Joy." I loved being her "Joy." Other days, Mom had these terrible headaches she called "dizzy spells." They left her depleted and defeated. On the bad days, my mom experienced a lot of physical and emotional pain. That's when I'd find her lying on the couch. Sometimes she stayed there for a few hours. Other times she'd remain there for days. Since the ups and downs were totally random, there was no knowing what the next moment might bring. She hung on in ways that pushed her physical and emotional limits. I figured only God could fuel such determination. How else did she find the strength to keep fighting?

My mom and dad liked to dance together. The memory of watching them dance is a taste of God. I can still imagine them smiling at each other as they danced. My dad would look at my mom with delight. My mom would look at him with adoration. On the bad days they still danced. I was sure there was a God who helped them keep on dancing.

I have some very simple memories of special people. I remember that my big sister always carried this magic canvas bag with her. It was filled with little gifts for me. I can still taste the potato chips that my oldest brother shared with me. I can still imagine the times I'd sit on the bed with him and watch TV. When I feel sand between my toes, the good times my brother, Gerald, and I enjoyed together at the shore flood my memory. These are all little bits and pieces of my past but they are well worth "remembering." They may seem like no big deal but they are. I felt love, protection and friendship in each moment. I felt God.

All these ways I came to know God I can take no credit for. I didn't even know enough to look for Him. God was the one who found me. Big looming churches, moody nuns, some man on a cross, music boxes, nakedness and some bread I'd eat after saying "Amen" made for some odd foundations of faith. Yet they made me aware of God at a very early age. I also knew Him through the beauty of my backyard, being chosen as Mary for my school Christmas pageant, in the kindness of my father, in shared potato chips, magic bags, sandy beaches and in the special ways special people have had The Touch. Endless moments that He has been real for me pour into my memory. "Remembering" God's first touches has been effortless and wonderful.

I've still got to give you more than I have. "Remembering" has been wonderful, but it's just the beginning of my story. It only offers a canvas that is spattered with hazy detail, lacking in vibrancy of color and full of much untouched white space. Incomplete, it is a story that offers little encouragement to others. To honestly offer my life as a gift, I must truly offer it: deeply, honestly and completely. From beginning to end, I now share my ordinary life. I share it with the prayer that my simple story will be an encouragement to others. This is my greatest hope. It's my purpose for sharing my journey.

Offer Your Life

Beginning

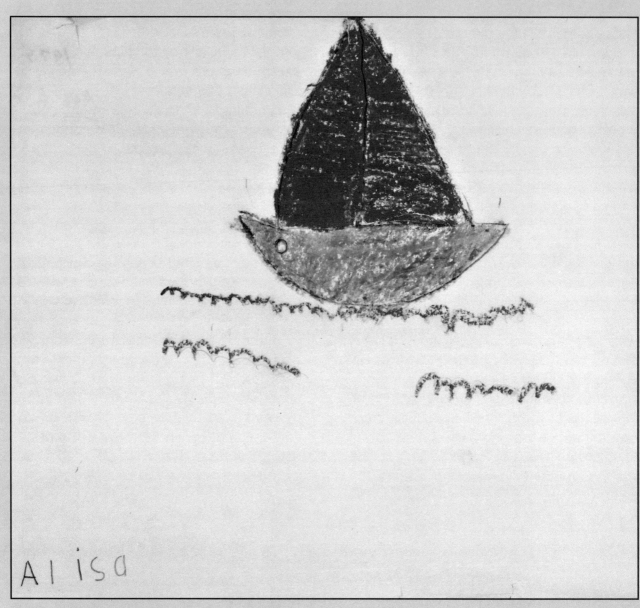

Setting Sail, Age 6

I'm at the kitchen table in my family room. I'm making a picture. It's a picture of a red and blue boat on the water. My mom is lying on the couch in the room with me. She doesn't feel well and I know it. It makes me sad. I want her attention. I know how to get it. I pick up my drawing and bring it over to her. "Mommy," I say. "Look what I made." She looks at my picture and smiles. She tells me that she likes what I made. Her words make me feel special. I believe I am an artist because my mom says that I am one.

My mom is an artist too, but she doesn't make her art on paper like me. Mom is a decorator and her favorite place to decorate is inside our home. In my house there are a lot of big rugs with fancy designs on them. The rugs are worn, and they're prickly when you sit on them. Today the house is cold, so I'm sitting on a pretty, prickly rug instead of on the floor. All around me are designs: designs on the rugs, designs on the bedspreads and designs on the wallpaper. My mom loves designs, patterns and colors. Some of the walls in our house don't have designs, but they're painted funny colors. My dining room has pink walls and a big fancy carpet that's really big. The way my mom decorates our home is wonderful.

I want to make a picture about our wonderful home. I draw a vase. I put flowers on the vase. I draw a gray flower, a green flower, a blue flower and an orange flower. The flowers make a nice design on the vase like the designs I see around me. I color the walls behind the vase a funny color. I choose orange. Orange goes good with the fancy vase with the flower designs. I like it. I think my mom will like it too.

At school we only get manila paper and crayons to make pictures during art class. Yesterday was special. We got finger paint. My art teacher is a nun. She wears a funny black and white outfit. She's not very friendly and she never says she likes anything anyone makes. She never talks to any of us. She's really old and doesn't usually like what I make like my mom does.

We were supposed to make a squishy mess with the blue finger paint. That's what the art teacher told us to do. I didn't want to make a squishy mess. I wanted to make a picture. I hoped my teacher would like it and she'd finally notice me. I made a house and a sunny sky with my blue finger paint. I added a tree. I was very happy. When the teacher came towards me I was excited to show her what I had made. She came to my desk and yelled at me for not following directions. She put her hand on my picture and made it into a squishy mess. Then she walked away. My teacher was angry with me.

At home I have good stuff for making art. I have more than crayons and manila paper. I have pastels, watercolors and clay my mom made me out of flour and water. I can make whatever I want and no one will get angry with me. What I make is encouragement for me. It promises me that Angry Art Teacher is wrong; what I make does matter, what I have to say matters and who I am matters. My creation tells me to keep being me, and to keep sharing what's me with others, and I listen. I'm going to be who I've got to be and give what I've got to give. It's the only way I know how to live. I've got to be me.

The One Left Behind, Age 9

I'm staying at Ya Ya's. Ya Ya lives on 177 East 75th Street in Manhattan. You would think that two weeks in the city would be exciting for me but it's not. I don't get to leave Ya Ya's that much. I'm stuck inside her two-bedroom apartment most of the time. It's OK being here, but I get really bored. My family is at the beach for a vacation. They say I'm too small for the 10-foot waves. That's their reason for having me stay at Ya Ya's. I miss my family. I don't really get why I couldn't go with everyone. I'm a really good swimmer. Maybe I was left out because there wasn't enough room in the station wagon for me? Along with two weeks' worth of luggage, my mom and dad brought along my sister, two brothers, my cousins and the dog. Where would I have fit in?

I'm lonely while everyone is having fun at the shore. There are many hours filled with nothing for me to do. To pass the time, I look out the window in Ya Ya's living room. I'm up really high; you have to take an elevator to get to her apartment. The cars below look like little toy cars. The buildings are big and dreary. The sky is gray. There isn't any grass, or trees, or flowers: only asphalt. I count the taxis. I reach 200. My breath leaves steamy marks on the window. I want to be with my family at the beach. I'm lonely.

I don't like to be lonely. I like to be with people. When people smile at me it feels good. I like it when people like what I say and do. I work really hard to please people, so that they like to have me around. I give people what they want and need. This is a good way for me to make sure that I have friends so that I'm not alone.

It matters to me that people like me. When people don't like me I feel sick in my gut. My tummy feels squirmy, my hands sweat and my throat feels tight. I do my best not to make people angry or frustrated, so I don't have to feel sick inside. People don't like it when I say or do the wrong things. That's why I pay close attention to what people say and do, so I can figure out what they want from me. Then I give them what they want so they're happy, or at least they don't yell at me as much.

Sometimes people are annoyed with me no matter what I do. I'm afraid of the annoyed people. My favorite people are the ones who are easy to please. With them I feel good and safe. I don't have to try so hard to be liked. When I'm with my favorite people, feeling alone seems far away.

I apologize a lot. Apologizing is my habit. I am the I'm Sorry Girl. I apologize even when I'm not sure what I did wrong. When I apologize what I'm really saying is, "I'll do my best not to make you angry again." Two of my friends got in a fistfight. They said that their fight was in my defense. I'm pretty sure they were just angry with each other, and I was their excuse to be angry. I don't tell them what I think, and I don't choose sides. Instead, I just do my best to make both of my friends happy with me. I do this by apologizing again and again. I don't need people to defend me. I just need them to like me and not be annoyed with me. That's why I say, "I'm sorry."

One angry girl is unhappy with me. She

wanted me to choose sides and defend her. I'm not sure it's right to choose sides, but I apologize for not having done so. She's still angry. I just keep saying, "I'm sorry. I'm sorry. I'm sorry."

Really, I'm a coward. The truth is that I'm not sorry. I believe Angry Girl picked the fight for her own reasons. Angry Girl thinks I'm a traitor, but the truth is I'm a wimp. If I was honest she'd hate me, and I can't handle the thought of that. That's why I act like a wimp. I'm afraid of her anger. I'll do just about anything to please her, so I can still count her among my friends. When I have friends I don't have to worry about being alone. I please people for their friendship and acceptance.

A pencil and a piece of white paper help me feel safe. When I make pictures I remember that I have a gift that gets me noticed. People are pleased when they see what I make. Sometimes, when I create, many people notice me at once. It feels good to be noticed. It feels very good.

I think people notice what I make because it's worth noticing. I make pictures about important things: beautiful things, memories and people and places worth remembering. Each picture is a story about something good. Sometimes when people look at my pictures they remember their own important things. When my gift makes someone remember like that it's better than good. It's awesome.

I trust that good memories are the stuff that God is made of. I can see Him in the good stuff: our wonderful home, the en-couragement of my mom, in my drawings and through the warm smiles of my favorite people. The ordinary, everyday "little things" God is made of are what make me happy. They let me see past Angry Girls, squishy messes, moody nuns and lonely days in my grandma's apartment. These "little things" are God's encouragement in the hard stuff. They are hope. I don't want to just keep the "little things." I want to share them so people will see the hope that I see. What I make with a pencil, on a piece of white paper, is a chance to show someone else what I see. It's a chance that the "little things" will make a difference.

Take the Chance

Being in "LUV", Age 12

I'm 12 years old. I'm at a seventh grade dance. I'm wearing a white miniskirt with red polka dots. A black and white striped top reaches over the top of the skirt. As the red polka dots meet with the black and white stripes you can't help but notice me. Getting noticed is the point. I want boys to notice me. I want the popular girls to like me. I feel awkward in my skinny and gangly body. My silver braces fill my smile, and my glasses highlight the nose my face hasn't quite yet grown into. I want to be seen, but I'm so afraid of being rejected. I'm afraid because I know I'm a dork.

There's a boy in my class that I really like. He's really cute. Because I'm a dork I figured I didn't have a chance with him. Donna is popular and the boys think she's pretty. Donna told me that I'd be pretty, and Cute Boy might like me, if I lost some weight. Figuring becoming skinny might be my avenue to popularity and a date with Cute Boy, I made my twelfth summer my summer to diet. After reaching my goal of 20 pounds lost, I felt fantastic. Surely Cute Boy and everyone else would notice me now. I had completely changed myself. I was skinny, tan and had a new haircut. I even had new knee-hi socks that stayed up around my calves instead of rolling down at my ankles. I had it all together, or so I thought. I was done being a dork and I was ready to be noticed.

No one noticed. No one said a thing. I was completely invisible throughout my first day of seventh grade. I lost 20 pounds and no one, my few close friends aside, had a compliment to extend or a kind word to speak. My summer of change left every-thing unchanged. I didn't matter and I remained unseen.

I'm the same person I was last year. I'm not prepared to be the same person. At 3:30 p.m., I make my way home on the big yellow bus. With a heavy pile of books, and sucking back the tears, I walk into the kitchen hoping for a hug. I find my mom, tired and sick on the couch watching television. I so want a glass of milk and some cookies from a mom with an apron and a smile. Instead, I sit with my broken mom, on the couch, and watch meaningless television about happy people with happy lives. I'm not like the happy people. I'm a dork without a hug. I'm very sad.

I'm definitely not "cool." I trip on my oversized feet and I still play with my dollhouse. I blush and my hands get clammy when a boy even gets near me. My mom still cuts my hair Dorothy Hamill style, and my shoes are from the bargain rack at the Salvation Army. My uniform is wrinkled and there's lots of cat hair on it. The popular girls have uniforms with crisp pleats, and if they have cats you can't tell by inspecting their garments. I spend my school days pulling up my knee socks because the elastic has stretched out of them. The boys like the girls with the nice and new knee socks, clogs and designer jeans. I had a pair of designer jeans once. They got stolen out of the girls' bathroom during cheerleading tryouts. They weren't even a day old. Even if I have a "cool" moment it doesn't last.

I romanticize about love. I make a Valentine's Day card for my mom and dad. I spell love with the letters "LUV." I fill the page with hearts and flowers. I imagine the first boy I will date will become my "LUV"ing husband. I want to be in "LUV" like my mom and dad. I think that being 12 and dating is all about "LUV."

I romanticize about a new boy at school. I imagine being in "LUV" with him. I imagine that he's in "LUV" with me. I want to dance with New Boy at my seventh grade dance. The DJ plays a slow song. My heart is racing and my hands are trembling. I walk up to New Boy and speak the words "Would you like to dance?" New Boy won't dance with me. Instead, he dances with another girl. She's a nice girl but she needs the adult-sized uniform so it will reach around her waist. I'm hurt and bewildered. Inside my head I say, "Even the chubby girl gets to dance tonight. What's wrong with me?"

Puberty is a nightmare. I'm the only girl in school who is not wearing a training bra and using a razor to shave her legs. Deodorant is a necessity that evades me as well. I start washing my face constantly to battle the pimples. I might have better results if I used Clearasil instead of Ivory Soap. The anxiety is the worst part. I'd always been an anxious kid but the new demands of adolescence make me tenser. Now I have a host of new things to worry about: boys, popularity, acne, razors, bras, dances, rejection and so much more.

I want to be noticed but the idea of being noticed makes my chest tight and my mouth dry. I still lie awake at night, but now I lie awake with my head spinning. I think of all the bad things that could happen to me that the "cool kids" might see. I could walk out of the bathroom with toilet paper stuck to my shoe. I could say something stupid in front of New Boy. I could get chosen last again in gym class. I daydream at night too. I imagine that I'm popular and I have a date. I imagine that my date and I fall in "LUV." I think about the new miniskirt I could save my money to buy. Maybe the new miniskirt would get someone to notice me? I realize it's not enough to please people anymore. Now, to be liked and noticed, I have to look and play the part. I can't figure out what part I'm supposed to play or how on earth I'm supposed to play it. It's hard to be a 12 year-old dork.

People don't notice me but I think God sees me. I hear Him inside me. He's that voice that says I matter. I'm not a dork to Him. I think He wants me to figure out how to play the part He meant me to play: a girl with a picture to make and a story to tell. Maybe if I play my part I'll encourage others to do the same. I'd like to figure out who I am and share who I am with others. Maybe I could even help others to share too? Then I'll have found a way for my life to make a difference.

Make a Difference

Heaven, Age 13

I have good friend I met in the seventh grade. Her name is Maureen. Maureen's parents like me. Her mom has become my spiritual mama. Mrs. Clark talks to me about God. She reads her Bible all the time and tells me that Jesus is her friend. I don't know how she knows Jesus like that, but I'm hoping she can help me know Him like that too.

Every year I get to go to the ocean with Maureen's family. Their beach house is a short walk from the shore, making the trip extra wonderful. I'm excited about the days at the shore, but I worry about the nights. I'll have to be quiet and careful not to disturb anyone. That means I'll have to lie in the dark and wait for the day to come. I'll try begging Jesus for sleep to come, but that doesn't usually change things. Knowing He is there does help though. I'm never completely alone in the dark and that is good. Besides, waiting in the dark for the days at the beach is worth it. In the mornings my head will hurt and my body will be tired. I'll enjoy the foamy sea anyway. I'll find shells and sea glass to make necklaces. The warm sun will feel good, and the long walks on the beach will make it feel like God is really close.

Today I want to think about the good things. I think about good things like the gift of a wonderful week at the beach. The ocean feels like Heaven. I love to swim in it. I'm a strong swimmer. I stroke hard and fast, and it feels awesome. I sense my bare feet on the damp sand, and I imagine that I don't have braces anymore. I imagine how my smile will look when the metal is gone along with my overbite. I look at my tan skin and wonder at its contrast against my white bikini. I enjoy how the salty sea agrees with my complexion, making it clear and smooth. As the sun shines on my face, I indulge the fantasy that I have the body of a woman instead of the body of a pre-pubescent. I revel in an occasional glance from a boy walking by me on the shore. Today I'm not a dork and that is good. It's a wonderful taste of good things and good things to come.

Today I stuff away the pain. I stuff away the pain of sleepless nights, acne, angry people, metal mouth and my exhausted head that pounds inside me. I paint the ocean and its foam. I make all the colors that surround me. I enjoy my new and very safe friend. I remind myself of all I have and all the promises of good things to come. Today it's not really hard to be happy.

My tomorrows will be different. I'm now a freshman dork at Albertus Magnus High School. Most of the kids from Saint Augustine's are joining me at Albertus, so it's not a fresh start. I get to bring my reputation as a dork along with me. All the Saint Augustine's kids will make sure everyone knows about who I was last year. There will be no new beginnings for me.

At home I don't have to worry about where I belong. I'm free from my social status. I'm free to be who I am there and I'm free to create. When I last got back from vacationing with Maureen I was eager to create. I painted the sea as the sun set. I remembered how wonderful it felt to be at the sea. I thought of how it felt to have gritty sand between my toes. I breathed in deeply to recall the faint smell of coconut from the tanning lotion I used to darken my skin. I imagined what I saw when I closed my eyes in the sun. Bright oranges, blues and deep yellows had filled the space behind my eyelids when I closed them. I don't just paint what I saw when the sun set. I also paint how it felt when I saw it. It felt like Heaven.

Luckily, I don't have to go back to the ocean for a taste of Heaven. My dad and my Aunt Julie planted and nurtured us our own little piece of Heaven right in our very own backyard. Loving to garden together, they shared an enjoyment for natural beauty and a patience to reap the benefits of the little things of life. They painstakingly grew a wide variety of fanciful goodies with packets of seeds, flower bulbs, some flats, a trowel and a watering can. Aunt Julie planted pungent white and purple irises all about our yard. Together, Dad and Aunt Julie started a vegetable garden that birthed big, tasty beefsteak tomatoes. They also planted rose bushes. Some had little pink roses and others had big red ones.

My mom liked the roses. She still does. She likes to say to my dad, "All I want is one rose." In my dad's garden is a rose-bush. He likes to go to the garden to clip the roses. Not all at once, though. One at a time, because that's the way my mom likes to get them. My dad brings each rose inside, and places it in a vase in the center of the kitchen table. Even when things are really bad, my dad keeps bringing my mother roses. Even when my mom doesn't feel well, the roses make her happy. They make me happy too.

Remembering is important to me. That's why I draw a picture of one rose, in a vase, in the middle of our kitchen table. I believe my drawing has power because it tells a story of hope where there should be none. My rose speaks words of encouragement in a world where encouragement is desperately needed. My drawing tells the truth: "One rose in a vase is the simple, ordinary goodness life is made of." What I have made tells my story with the hope that it might give hope to someone else. It's the chance for someone else to see the goodness life is made of. It's also an invitation for someone else to share in return.

One Rose, Age 14

Share In Return

No Place Like It, Age 17

Thank God. Thank God I finally have a boy-friend. I was so full of anticipation on Friday night when I met Cameron. Allen Parsons Project played on the hi-fi in the living room as the party started. The music was new to me and I liked the sound of it. I liked Cameron too. I noticed him right away when he entered the house. I couldn't imagine a boy like Cameron liking me.

A bunch of us all lay on the floor next to the fireplace being goofy and listening to the music. I was downright giddy with anticipation. Cameron was next to me. He reached over and held my hand. I was so excited I thought I might pass out. His hand felt so good wrapped around my fingers. My hair stood up on my arms and I felt a wave of warmth pass through my entire being. The moment had finally arrived. Someone wanted me.

Being wanted was good but it added something new to my worry list: kissing. I felt so stupid being 17 and having no idea how to kiss. I figured it was best to come clean and just tell Cameron that I had never done this kissing thing before. He assured me that he had it all together and that we'd do just fine. He was enough of a gentleman. I got past my anxieties. It was awkward and embarrassing at first. I eventually settled down some. I even enjoyed myself a little bit. I had survived the first kiss. What a relief.

Returning home from my date felt awkward. It was very late. I quietly slinked in the back door. I thought my dad might tell what had transpired by the look on my face and the hour of my return. Being a little em-barrassed, I hoped to dodge him. Dad was waiting, though. He was patiently waiting my return. I found him nodding off slightly in his rocking chair in the T.V. room. He smiled and greeted me. Then he went off to bed. I noted the generosity in his readiness to let me grow up. I noted his willingness to let me face the perils and perks of becoming a woman. "He knows," I thought. "He knows that I've been kissed."

I went to bed excited and relieved and actually woke up refreshed. I was aware that it had been two weeks, maybe more, since I had slept through the night. I stretched, yawned and crawled out of bed to face a new and more hopeful day. Pausing on my way to the bathroom to look out the window, I noted that the view was cause for pause. It was beautiful. I saw the six big apple trees in my backyard. They were full of green leaves and apples. I saw big open spaces full of sunshine, green grass and bright yellow dandelions. There were apples falling to the ground everywhere. A deer and some rabbits had come to eat them. The beauty was starker than usual. It was starker against the backdrop of the wonder and hope sparked by my first kiss and the possibility of being loved. I noticed that, in little bits and pieces, I was outgrowing this place called my childhood home. I knew that I wanted to remember this day, and this beautiful view, when the day came that I would have to leave. I try to make a picture that captures the beauty of what I see from my bedroom window. I feel both sad and exhilarated as I paint. I want to keep what I see. Yet, on this day, I'm a little more ready to let it go.

God gave me a gift. I make some really good art with my gift. It captures the goodness of my life. Some people are comforted by the pictures of the good things I make. Everyone doesn't notice that I have a gift, though. It's often overlooked or undervalued. I figure it's a gift that has value or God wouldn't have given it to me. I don't think He makes the mistake of giving people gifts that don't matter. I'm an artist and it matters. My life matters.

It's my senior year in high school. It's time to decide on a college and Pratt is hosting a portfolio day. I've selected my best work and I've put it behind the plastic sleeves in my big black portfolio case. I put my transcripts and letters of recommendation in an envelope. My dad and I drive to Brooklyn, NY. I get in line to show my portfolio to an advisor. I'm accepted on the spot and I'm excited. Pratt is just about the best art school there is. It's where I'm really going to learn to use my gift.

I'm finding there's still plenty to be anxious about since I've decided where I'll spend my freshman year of college. The No Sleep Cycle is what makes me most anxious. I feel some anxiety, I can't sleep and then I feel anxious (because I'm exhausted) so I can't sleep. I hate to admit it, but I do worry a lot. The anxiety isn't strong enough to squelch the urge, though. It's the urge to create and share what I create. It's the urge to be an artist who has something good to share.

Being an artist makes me different from my peers. Most of the kids at Albertus come to school with a backpack, a polo shirt and penny loafers over their argyle socks. I dress differently. I wear high black boots, with zippers and snaps, over black nylons. My earrings are big, ornate and wonderfully odd. Around my neck hangs a necklace with rhinestones and pearls. In my hand is my big black case full of art. I used to be embarrassed trudging down the halls of Albertus Magnus High School with my big, dorky portfolio case. Now I'm proud that I'm an artist. I can't help but make art. The urge to make is too strong inside of me. It's more painful to try and fit in than it is to be myself. I'm finally brave enough to start being me.

Right now, I have the urge. I create. I draw a tree. It's an apple tree like the ones at home in my backyard. This apple tree has lost its fruit and leaves, yet it's a tree of encouragement. This tree I draw is a tree that, after the fall and winter, will burst forth with green leaves and bear new fruit. The tree, like me, does what it was created for. It changes and grows as it was intended to. What an incredible world this would be if we, like my tree, each lived the life we were meant to live and then shared our story.

Tree of Encouragement, Age 17

Learning

Simple Truth, Age 19

Dad and I ride the elevator to the 16th floor of Willoughby Hall with some of my things to make me feel at home at Pratt. I laugh inside as I look at my dad in the elevator, with his blue and yellow plaid pants on, standing between a boy with purple hair and a bald woman with tattooed arms. At home things are much different from Pratt's open campus in the middle of Brooklyn. What's most different is the people. The people at Pratt are pretty wild. I used to think I could be a little wild. I used to drink some at my friends' backyard tent parties during high school. I smoked clove cigarettes when I drank and even tried pot once. I took one drag. It wasn't even enough to get a head rush. I felt naughty. At Pratt you can be wild and have lots of good company. Drugs are available if you want them. You barely have to ask. Wine is on our kitchen counter. Beer is in the fridge. Two girls down the hall are having sex with each other. I'm scared of the guy who lives on the 14th floor. He wears all black clothing, has tattoos of Hell on his arms and he stares at me.

I don't like to drink. It gives me a headache. I don't want to do drugs. I'll just get addicted and have another problem to overcome. I'm having enough trouble finding a guy to fall in love with. I don't need to add trying to love a woman to the mix. Hell scares me. I don't want to be alone with the guy who wears pictures of Hell on his arms. At my high school I was the weird, dorky art chick who was deemed the nutty one. At Pratt I'm the controlled, conventional, and scrupulous one. That's OK with me and it's OK with my friends too. I'm comfortable here. We're all different and we like it. It's ironic. For the first time I feel like I really belong.

At Pratt I belong, but I still have plenty of problems. My mom had problems when she was young too. Mom tried a lot of different things to help her feel better. She went to some doctors for help with her headaches. The doctors ran tests but they didn't find anything wrong. Mom was tired a lot so they poked around for reasons why. They didn't find any reasons. She tried a bunch of diets, and energy drinks, to help with her "dizzy spells." None of these efforts made much of a difference for her. Regular visits to an osteopath helped some. She seemed to feel better for a day or two after these appointments but she still hurt. Her muscles hurt. She tried exercises and stretches to relieve the discomfort. It helped a little. Everything Mom asked for help with became a problem that got worse over time. I can identify with how my mom felt when she couldn't find answers. Like me, she reached out for help but the help she got was never enough.

My problems are somewhat different than my mom's. My biggest problem is that I still can't sleep. Like it was for my mom, finding answers to what is happening to me is looking unlikely. I want to be healthy but my journey towards health is littered with imperfect solutions and dead end efforts. And, like my mom, I just keep getting sicker. I sleep for only short periods of time. I have incredible headaches. After a bad night, my head will pound deep inside my skull. My whole body aches from muscle tension. I have a chronic cough. I'm constantly on antibiotics. I feel dread when I'm really tired. It's the anxiety of my youth multiplied by 10. Eventually, I have a good night and I feel some relief. Then, the No

Sleep Cycle continues.

My life is a mixed bag. Not being able to sleep is a bad thing, but my life has so many good things. I see the good stuff that is mixed in with the bad. I see the beauty in the mixed bags. I search for the beautiful moments hidden in places where others might find only darkness. That's why I make art that's about the light. Some of my classmates recreate darkness. They make scary art. It's scary to me, anyway. I don't want to make scary art. I'm too busy looking for the beautiful moments and the good stuff. These are the moments I want to capture on my canvas.

Today I'm painting a simple truth: flowers are beautiful. I think about all the beautiful flowers from the backyard of my childhood. I recall the color of the petals and the ways they twisted, folded and bended. I think about the garden creations of my dad and Aunt Julie. In my mind I see little pink roses and baby deer eating tiny green crab apples that dropped in the grass. I remember the taste of the sour green apples and the smell of the white and purple irises. I recall the feeling of cold dew on my feet as I walked on the grass in early morning. The beauty around me is good stuff and I paint it. No matter what happens to me, or others, this is one beautiful world. No one can take its beauty away from me.

I'm seeing a counselor because I want to sort through my mixed bag life. I think she can help me heal the dark places and shine the light more brightly on the beautiful moments. I'm hoping she can help me sleep better, too. I figure she might be able to help me relax. Then I should find that I am able to rest better. That's why my counselor and I talk about what has happened, and is happening, in my life. If I can soften my anxieties maybe I will be able to close my eyes and drift off to sleep like everyone else?

My counselor shows me that I don't have to accept the bad stuff that has been believed about me or the negative thoughts I have about things. I start to believe that I'm not really a dork at all. I start to enjoy my own uniqueness. I begin to see that I'm worth loving. I stop measuring my worth by how many dates I've had or whether a boy likes me. Some days I look in the mirror and see someone really pretty. On a good day, I recognize that if someone doesn't want to dance with me it's their loss. I have a new way of seeing my big, black portfolio case and the unconventional ways of my high school years. I no longer think that I was a spectacle or something to be gawked at and studied with disbelief. Today I see a different Alisa: a wonderful spectacle who is interesting, vibrant and full of life.

In counseling I sort out the fears, sadness and disappointments that come with having a mom who hurts. I'm sad when I think about what's happening to my mom. I don't want her to be sick. I don't want my dad to have to see her like this. What's happening to my mom is really terrible, but my counselor helps me sort my worries. She shows me that I don't have to be so afraid. Today my thoughts are less anxious. It's a relief.

In counseling I start to understand the truth about my sadness. I see that some of my sadness comes because of the good things. In counseling I see that I have good reasons to love people, and it's natural for me to feel sadness when I see them in pain. One of my good things is being Looby Loo. That's my mom's nickname for me. When she uses it, she says it sweetly. I love being Looby Loo. It's also one of the reasons why it's so hard for me to see my mom hurt. It's hard when some of the people you love most are in pain.

I refuse to give up the good things. No matter how sick my mom or I get, I will hang on to nostalgia, memories and wonderful moments with fierceness. I will love broken, sick and struggling people. I will embrace people who are different than me and I will love the ways they are unique. I will love God, and see Him everywhere, even though I have problems. I will find meaning in the big moments and the little, ordinary ones. The gift of being the storyteller of one's own life is freedom. It's the freedom to choose everything: the details, meanings, purposes and power of every moment lived. Right now I continue to choose. I choose to hold on to the good things because they encourage me, and others, to see the beauty of life. I share these things because I can. It's my life.

It's Good to Share

So Naive, Age 19

I go on this date and it's not a good thing. I'm so excited. I'm so naïve. This guy and I go out to dinner and then back to his apartment. I'm thinking we're going to watch television, cuddle and maybe kiss a little. That's not what happens. Instead, my date turns into Disgusting Guy. He gets off while I stare at the dirty wall by the bed. Grimy fingerprint marks and big chunks of chipping paint covered it. I crossed my arms over my body to protect myself and just looked away while he got some of what he wanted. I leave Disgusting Guy's dorm room feeling nauseated and foolish, but knowing I was lucky.

I knew I was lucky because I fought Disgusting Guy off enough to keep my clothes on and keep my virginity. I felt far from lucky, though, on the inside. Inside I was feeling dirty. I figured feeling dirty was part of what happens when someone uses you as their scratching post. Still, I was disgusted with myself for letting it go as far as it did. "It could have been so much worse. I could have lost so much more," I say to myself. I look at my watch. I realize it's Valentine's Day. I want to cry. "There will be no flowers for me today," I say inside myself. "I wish there was someplace, or something, that would make me feel good again."

I take a shower, cry and pull myself together a little. I take out my paints so I can get lost in them. I try to forget what happened for a little while. I try to remember how I felt about myself just yesterday. I remember how innocent and unassuming I was. I paint some flowers. I use sweet pink, pale yellow and soft green. I realize that I could paint something really dark. I've had a dark

night. I feel the darkness all around me. Still, what I paint is as simple and unassuming as I was yesterday. I can go back to being five years old if I want to. I can paint like a child if I'd like. I'm Looby Loo again if I choose. I want to paint innocence, not innocence lost. I've lost some innocence. I paint to get it back.

My date is more than bad. It has revived forgotten pieces of my past. They're not good pieces. Bad Date stirs up bad memories. I remember that I was hurt in the past. I recall bits and pieces of how I got touched. I remember I was touched in ways I shouldn't have been. I recall how the touching happened at different times and in different ways. The person who hurt me wasn't always the same. Each event, in itself, was not terrifically significant. All the events in combination, though, add up to what happened on Gross Date. I never learned how to say no. I've got the boundaries of a five-year-old.

Since Gross Date, I feel stirred up. My gut is tight and it lurches when I think about what happened that night. I tell my counselor, "There's something wrong with me. I don't like the boys I date." I share my memories and the details of my date gone bad. I ask my counselor if she thinks that I have a problem. She says, "Everyone has problems," and she challenges me to keep facing them. Her advice seems right to me, so I take it.

With all my problems, I have an important job on campus. I'm a resident advisor. I help people in spite of the fact that I need so much help. I live in the freshman dormitory and I help 16 of the freshman girls as they adjust to college living. I love my job. I don't just like art. I like people. I like helping people. Resident advisors get to do lots of helping. I'm learning to help in good ways. Sometimes helping in the right ways means that I don't please people or give them what they want. I have a tough time with this part of my job, but I know I can't do my job right if I'm always trying to make everyone happy. Last week I noticed that one of the girls on my floor is cutting class and she has a drinking problem. She's going to be angry when I confront her, but I can't turn a blind eye to what she's doing. She's in trouble and she's my responsibility.

I have a habit of carrying around other people's feelings. When friends are sad, I feel sad. I cringe around angry people. When someone is sick I feel terrible. Sometimes,

I think I fix people so I can feel better. Other times, I think it's good to help people and it's natural to want to help them. I'm really good at helping people. I talk to the girl with the drinking problem. It's rough going at first, but she sees what I'm trying to do. She knows that I want to help her. She lets me help.

I want to help. That's why I've decided to become an art teacher. It's the perfect job for me. I can help kids make art. I can help teach kids to make art that means something to them. Maybe I could show children how art can help them tell their story? Maybe I could teach them to share? Then their lives would really make a difference. Together, our lives could make a difference.

It's Good to Help

Speak, Age 20

My counselor has been replaced. The new counselor gives me a sick feeling in my gut when she gives me advice. I thought counselors were supposed to listen and help you come to your own conclusions. That's not what New Counselor does. She makes lots of suggestions, especially when it comes to boys. New Counselor thinks it would be great if I had sex with a good friend of mine. My friend is cute and nice, but I don't want to have sex with him. I'm not in love with him. I want to have sex with a man I'm in love with. New Counselor thinks that the love part will come later for me. I'm confused.

New Counselor has other ideas. Because of my limited sexual experience, she believes that I might be a lesbian. Now I'm really confused. I walk out of New Counselor's office and I want to cry. It's early evening and a storm is coming in. The sky matches my emotions; it's dark, tumultuous and swirling. My throat feels really tight and cold drops of rain hit my face as I walk across the campus. I imagine my life without a man. I imagine my life as a lesbian. I cry because I want children and a husband really badly, and I'm afraid that these things might not be for me. I consider what the truth is. "Am I a lesbian?" I ask myself. "Am I attracted to women?"

I see that Pratt is one of the safer places on earth to be a lesbian. I'm sure my family and friends would accept me regardless of my sexual preference. I think of how nice it felt to hold Cameron's hand and how good it felt to kiss my Valentine's Eve date before the date got gross. I try to transfer those feelings to a woman. I think, "I don't want my life if it's going to be spent with a woman."

I see New Counselor for a few more sessions. Finally, I decide to follow my gut and I stop meeting with her. Part of me worries that I'm running from the truth that New Counselor is trying to make me see. Most of me is pretty sure she's wrong about the truth. My gut says, "There are things you're afraid of, Alisa, but you're not a lesbian. It's not something you are or are going to become. Don't be afraid. Stand on your own. Trust yourself." Today I'm learning to trust my gut.

Trusting my gut doesn't change the reality that everyone in the dormitory is sleeping but me. I keep falling asleep for a few minutes and waking up with my heart racing. I know it's useless to go back to bed. I'm too revved up now. I make the best of the extra time I have awake while everyone else is refueling. I paint from a photo of my parents' backyard. I paint the flowers in the photo with the hopes of capturing the beauty that surrounded me as a child. I want my canvas to show how my mixed bag life has still been full of many good things. I want it to tell my story. I want my canvas to speak.

If the painting did tell my story, what kind of story would it be? It might tell an ordinary story of a very tired girl whose rest was found in a God who knew what He was doing. It could speak of a God who helped her find joy in spite of how tired she was or how lonely she became. Her story might tell of victory, because the girl kept getting up every morning and living no matter how hard it was for her to live. If she still smiled and laughed every day, and if she kept her enthusiasm for many things, might her story encourage others to wake up and find joy? Then, the girl might find that her life has really been worth it. Then, she might come to realize that her simple, ordinary life had managed to find a way to speak.

My Voice, Age 21

I'm no longer the resident advisor of the freshman dorm. I'm the resident director. It's ironic that I'm the resident director. Two hundred freshman students live in the dormitory with me. I'm supposed to bring them stability, safety and predictability. It's amazing that I manage to do my job so well. I'm so messed up. It's a miracle that my life is any good for anyone.

At Pratt people are honest about their lives and they are not afraid to share. People know all about my troubles but they still come to me with theirs. We share life honestly. Sometimes I find that I'm the one who's holding things together. This happens even on the days when I feel like I'm falling apart.

It's 3 a.m., and I'm really tired. I drink some of the cold medicine I've collected from the extra freshman welcome packs. It makes me tired at first and I fall asleep, but I don't sleep for very long. I wake up a little while later with my heart pounding. I'm feeling sick and exhausted. I get up. It's useless to go back to bed. I'm too keyed up.

I turn on a lamp and work on a painting. I paint myself playing the flute. A friend gives me flute lessons in the chapel once a week. I'm learning to play songs from a hymnal. I can't sing very well so the flute is my voice. I try to paint how I feel when I'm playing hymns on my flute. I feel like I'm playing a song just for God, and He's watching me. I feel like He likes what He sees.

I leave my room to use the bathroom. I can hear one of the boys snoring through his dorm room door. I hate him for being able to snore. I hate him for being able to sleep. It feels like everyone in the world is sleeping but me. "Maybe I'll drink some more of the cold medicine. Maybe it will help for a little while?" I wonder. I don't even bother. I know it won't bring any relief. "It's useless," I say to myself. "There's nothing that will help me."

I go back to my painting. I lose myself in it. I forget how sick I feel. I forget how angry I am that I can't stay asleep. Sometimes forgetting is good. Sometimes forgetting is the best medicine that I have.

Forgetting can be good, but remembering can be good too. I think of a wonderful memory. I remember how my mom and my sister made a big fuss over me on Christmas. They took pictures of me wearing a fancy coat I had gotten as a gift. My sister put my hair up and did my makeup. My mom put a funky hat on my head. They took some more pictures. I looked at myself in the mirror. I looked beautiful. I felt beautiful.

I want to paint myself in my unusual coat. I use one of the Christmas coat photos my sister took to help me create. I put a crucifix around my neck even though I wasn't wearing one in the picture. The coat isn't really red but I make it red anyway. I like how I can do that. I like how I can change things when I paint. Sometimes I can tell the story better this way. I want to show how I felt. I want to show what's important to me. I want to show what's inside me and I want to share it with others. Every mark I make means something. Every mark helps me tell the story of what matters to me.

What matters now is that the world is full of hope and possibilities. It's time to graduate, and I'm excited. Maybe things will change for me now? Maybe I'll get a great job that lets me make a difference? I might really help some kids. I could build their confidence and help them know that they matter. Is it possible that I might sleep better now? Maybe living in the dorm has been too noisy for me and I just need a quieter place to rest? Maybe I'll meet a man who's a teacher? Then we'd both be interested in helping kids, so we'd have something important in common. That would be great. Perhaps the routine of a regular job will help me relax? Regular hours could agree with me and I could enjoy a simpler, and easier, life. It feels like anything is possible. I suspect that I'm a little too hopeful. There's so much that is still the same or even worse. My mom is worse. My sleep is worse. I still find myself worrying about things. I'm still alone. The only thing that remains the same is God and who He is for me. He's the only hope I can be sure of for tomorrow. He is what matters the most.

God really is all I've really got in this life, and He's all I've got to give to others. He's my encouragement and my encouragement to give. He's my reason to create, to tell and to share. He's my story. He's my life.

Let Others In

Searching

The Way It Used to Be, Age 22

I just finished swimming laps in the pool at the Field Club. It's the summer swim and tennis club our family joined when I was six years old. I'm only a visitor today, but I don't need to belong here to keep what once made this place great for me: the memories. The best memories are of the friends I had here. Like me, they don't come here very much anymore. The stuff that once made this place so wonderful has completely changed.

Late at night, when most people had left the club, I'd wait for my parents to finish partying with their friends. I'd wait in the club's gazebo with my sketch book and colored pencils. I remember how the walls of the gazebo made a funny shape and had hundreds of little windows. It had French doors leading to a side exit, and it held pretty little wrought-iron tables and chairs and a little wicker couch with a spongy cushion. All of this gave me something new to draw each time I waited. Today, the gazebo sits and waits for me to draw it again like I did when I was young. It is the same as it was when I was a child. It's one of the few things at the Field Club that hasn't changed.

I have some really good things happening in my life right now and that helps soften the blow of bittersweet change. I got my regular elementary teaching certificate. I'm teaching first grade and I really like it. I love building relationships with the kids and showing them that they have something good to share. I love my teaching job, but I'm exhausted at the end of the day. When I get home at 7 p.m., I quickly eat, grade some papers and go to bed to rest up for another busy day. I'd be handling all this

much better if I could get the rest I need. Instead, I'm still awake at night and I'm weary by the time morning comes. I'm sick a lot and I can't stop coughing. I've also become impatient with things that never used to bother me. Last week, a cashier was really slow, and very nasty, as she checked me out. She dug into me for using the express lane when I had 14 items instead of 12. My hands shook as Angry Cashier started berating me. Her face was red and angry. I felt red and angry inside. We made a fine pair.

I've completely lost patience for people who cut me off in traffic. I say nasty things to the faceless drivers. I don't like how I feel. The muscles in my shoulders and back are tight. I grit my teeth. I'm anxious. Mostly, I'm just very tired.

It's 3 a.m. I look at some old photos of myself. The photos make me think back to when I first saw that my life was different. It was when I saw the other moms hosting Brownie troop meetings and coming on class trips. It was when my mom tried to be a part of things, but her "dizzy spells" often kept her away. My photos jar the memory of how the nuns taught me about suffering. They taught me that suffering was a gift from God. I remember figuring that God must think my mom was really special to give her such a gift. I think, "Maybe He gave me The Gift too?"

I see myself as connected to my mom in her suffering. We're connected because we don't have any control over what's happening to us. We're also connected because it's not our fault, and we're connected because our suffering has no solution. It has no answers and it just gets worse.

I don't have "dizzy spells" but I have headaches that don't relent. Like my mom, I try to be a part of things, but when I'm exhausted I lose steam just like she did. I want to be the same mom that my mom wanted to be. I'd like to be the quintessential mom too, but instead I'm afraid I'll end up falling very short. My mom needed her "dizzy spells" to go away. She needed energy to get off the couch. I need to sleep and I need an escape from the pain in my head. In suffering, we're just not that different.

I dig back through my early memories. My memories show how "it" was subtle at first: "it" being how I was starting to be special too. I remember occasionally waking and having trouble falling back to sleep. That was when I was really little. When I was about 12, being awake in the dark became part of a rhythm. The photos remind me of when I started asking Jesus for a "normal" life. Things forgotten come to the surface. I see how, over a decade later, my nighttime world is an even greater place of torment. I still wake up all night long. I have terrible dreams. I often wake up screaming and sweating. My heart will be pounding within my chest, making it impossible for me to fall back asleep. Until my heart stops racing it's not even worth bothering to try closing my eyes. Sometimes I'll stay awake until the sun comes up. I'm too afraid to go back to bed because I know the nightmares will keep coming if I do. These are the worst nights because exhaustion hits early and with a heaviness that stays with me all the way through the next day. When the next night comes there's no guarantee that rest will come. In fact, it almost never comes.

The liquor cabinet brings temporary relief when the nights become unbearable. I drink just enough to drift off for a little while. I hate the taste of vodka, so I plug my nose and down a shot or two. It's ironic. I hate feeling drunk. At parties I'm always sober. I drive my friends home safely. I'm the responsible one. No one knows about my night-time salve. I keep it a secret. It's not worth sharing because the truth makes no difference. If I had other options I'd try them. I'm not an alcoholic. I'm just desperate.

Desperation sucks but it doesn't stop me from seeing the world as a place full of miracles. I believe in big miracles and little ones, and at the same time I'm sick. Being sick isn't a miracle. In fact, it's pretty awful sometimes. Some people look at my life as proof that miracles don't happen. I understand why so many people don't believe that miracles happen. They see so many people in pain that it's hard to believe. They're confused. Sometimes I'm confused too. When I think of the horror of concentration camps, or that I live in a world where children are tortured and abused, I get really confused. I start to lose my faith, and believing in miracles begins to seem foolish. That's when I begin to question whether the miracles I see are real. I hate that. I do my best to keep believing because my faith matters to me. It matters a lot. It's the glue that holds me together.

It's probably hard for people to understand

how I could still believe in miracles, but I do. I've spent my life waiting for the miracle of being healed so that I can sleep and have peace. Maybe I've misjudged what the "big miracle" is? Maybe Jesus has already answered me but He didn't do it in the way I thought He would? Perhaps the "big miracle" is that somehow I still believe in miracles. Miracles are the hope I have left and the hope I have left to give. They are the stuff my life is made of. In fact, they have become my story.

Give Hope

A Bed to Sleep In, Age 24

It should be no surprise that I hate beds. Even before I lie down, dread creeps in. Nothing brings me comfort. My childhood bed was made for a princess. It had soft cotton sheets, a beautiful antique wooden frame, and a warm floral comforter. I hated it. I hated the way the flowers on the wallpaper matched the sheets and blankets. I hated the soft pillows. I despised it all. I still despise it.

I'm sick of living like this. I really do need a miracle. I want to live like a normal person. I hate my smiling teacher friends with their rested bodies and beds that they can sleep in. I've been hanging on to hope for a lifetime, and I'm not sure how much longer I can hang on. It's hard for me to be happy. The smiles I wear are becoming forced. I'm so tired. I'm beyond exhausted, but I'm still believing in the day that I will be a normal, smiling teacher with a bed I can sleep in. I hold on for the day when the smiles that illuminate my face are genuine and joyful. Every night I ask Jesus to bring me this miracle. I still believe, against the evidence, that He hears me.

Jesus hears me. He's the greatest hope and encouragement my life has to give. You're wrong if you can't see the miracles. My life is a story of miracles: ordinary, wonderful, little miracles with some big, fantastic miracles mixed right in. I want the world to know they're real miracles. That's why I share the truth of my life and hope others will share the truth of their lives too. Maybe together we could show the world that we're surrounded by miracles? I'm tired of the lie that life is meaningless and that there's nothing good in this world to be found. My life is full of struggle yet I still see abounding goodness. When I tell my story I challenge others to see the goodness. Then I just hope. I hope that others will share their story too.

Challenge Others

Best Left Alone, Age 25

I've been dating the same man for about nine months now. He's not the one for me. When it comes to the opposite sex, little has changed for me since college. I'm dating, but I'm just going through the motions. I feel nothing romantic.

I want a partner who can make me feel safe. I don't feel very safe right now. In fact, I feel pretty sick to my stomach. My gut is acting up again. It's telling me that something isn't right. I'm going to listen to my gut.

I want someone I can spend my life with. I know my gut is right. I know this isn't the man God has for me. I've started to accept that I might be alone. I'm surprised to find how good it feels to start accepting it. I see it's better to be alone than to be with someone who is wrong for me. I prefer the loneliness.

My paints keep me company. I use them to give my loneliness a voice, so it can be understood. The brushstrokes don't lie. They paint the portrait of a woman whose life is lived alone. I'm a "me" aching to be an "us." For the first time, oddly, that's OK.

My students keep me company and they help make my life OK. I love my newest job as an elementary school teacher. My classroom is perfect and my students are bright and eager to learn. I enjoy the variety among all my students regardless of their abilities. We write plays, make books, film movies and go to the art room to make learning come alive. It's a fantastic time.

I get surprise evaluations from my principal and my superintendent. The evaluations are the antithesis of a fantastic time. My gut does somersaults every time my classroom door opens. I wish I didn't have to worry about what they think or when they're going to appear. It's too hard to please them all the time. They could walk in when I'm having a bad moment no matter how few bad moments I have. I should know that I'm a great teacher. Instead, I work to prove myself. If I had confidence, I'd know I was the best they could get. I'd make them work to keep me. I wouldn't grovel.

I'd love to be impervious to judgment and criticism. Instead, I feel the weight of what everyone wants and what everyone thinks of me. As long as I'm meeting everyone's expectations then everyone's pleased. To be pleasing I have to play the game of trying to figure out what everyone wants so I can give it to them. Then everyone is happy. Even I'm happy if I pretend hard enough.

I don't have to pretend on my canvas; I can be whoever I want to be, and do whatever I want to do. It's freedom to break the rules on my canvas. It doesn't fight back. It doesn't want anything from me. It's open to what I desire. It celebrates in my freedom. It gives me the chance to be really alive. It lets me step out of line and break out of the box. I don't have to pretend, and I decide what is pleasing. I have space to breathe and share. Sometimes, when I paint, I don't even feel alone.

My paints make me happy. It feels good to tell my story, even if it's the story of a woman who's alone. I'm grateful that I have a way of capturing what matters in my life. I love the fact that others can look at what I've made and see what matters. It's awesome when people see what I've made and it makes them start telling stories about their own lives. When they talk, sometimes they smile, or their eyes well up with tears. My life touched theirs. Their life touched mine. It's amazing.

Simple, Little, Wonderful Things, Age 25

Right now I'm trying to figure out a clean and fast way to break up with a guy. I can't stand another minute with him. I need to bolt.

My boyfriend hates his mother and he treats me like I'm less than him. Something about the way he treats me really gets under my skin. When he's near me I'm nauseous. When his skin touches mine my whole body recoils. I still let him touch me even though I don't want his touch. He has a way of breaking me down and making me weak. He feeds on my weaknesses. I don't like a lot about him but I've let him get to me. I've got to get away from him but I don't know how to begin. I feel so trapped.

I'm still keeping my virginity until I find someone that I love. I am so glad I didn't sleep with this man. Thank God I didn't let him be my first. I'd rather be a 25-year-old virgin than to have gained my first experience with someone who now makes my gut wrench. Thank God I didn't let him get to all of me. My virginity was one of the few boundaries I have left that he wasn't able to dissolve.

This relationship has reached in and grabbed at my vulnerabilities. I'm confused and full of fear. That's what the last six months have taught me. It's easy to yank me around. I'm like a dog on a leash. I can't go where I want to go. My biggest weakness is pride. I've been afraid to say some things. I'm afraid of what people will think of me once I say them. I think it's time I face my fears.

The truth is that I'm very afraid of something. I feel most afraid when I lie alone in bed at night. I stare out the window. I watch the moon light the trees from behind. The moon's glow projects the shadows of leaves flickering on the bedroom walls. Everything around me feels empty, cold and hopeless. I lie on my back, stare at the ceiling and wait to doze off. Counting to five thousand is accomplished. You're supposed to fall asleep while you're counting but I usually don't. It becomes clear that I might not sleep at all. This is the kind of night when the fear really gets at me. When it's dark and I'm alone and exhausted, I start to slip. Anxiety grabs me as I think ahead to what the next day has in store for me. I know the day is going to be a battle to keep it together in my exhaustion. I'm afraid I won't win the battle; it's the battle for my sanity. I'm too worn down to be sure I can escape my fear. It's the fear of becoming mentally ill.

I've been so afraid to admit how I fear mental illness. I fear it in a way that gives the fear power over me. When I hide in fear it's as though my anxieties grip me and trap me even more. When I get really tired, I sometimes feel like I'm riding the edge of insanity. I have to work really hard to fight my way back from the edge. What I'm afraid of matters a lot right now because my boyfriend's mom is mentally ill. I don't like the way my boyfriend treats his mom. I don't like the way his dad treats my boyfriend's mom either. My dad would never treat my mom like that no matter how mentally ill she got. I don't think I'm ready to be with someone who's going to treat me that badly if my fear of insanity is realized. I've got to get away. God, please help me get away.

I could end up like my boyfriend's mom if I stay in this relationship. My boyfriend could push me over the edge. Something about the way he treats me leaves me feeling small and powerless. My boyfriend recently told me that he believes electric shock therapy is a nifty solution for the sufferings of the mentally ill. He made it sound like the equivalent of taking pain medication for a hangnail. He told me how his mother has benefited from a few rounds of electric shock therapy. Something about the way he talks about his mother makes my throat burn and tighten. He makes his mother sound like one of the rats from my dad's lab. When my boyfriend talks about his mother, something hollers at me from within. I have a voice inside me that's screaming, "Get out!" Yet I don't trust my instincts. I keep looking for more reasons to get out. When am I going to realize that I have enough reasons to flee? When am I going to acknowledge my voice?

A chocolate cake becomes my reason to "Get out!" The chocolate cake was a gift for my boyfriend from his mother. He didn't thank her for the cake. He said his mother had nothing better to do than make it for him. I saw how angry he was with her. I know his life was no party. He had plenty of reasons to be resentful towards his mother. As his girlfriend, though, I had to consider what his resentment might end up meaning for me.

If I had married this man would I have ever been able to believe that I wouldn't be mentally ill? How many rounds of electric shock therapy would be required before life as a marginalized psychotic was all I knew? I doubt I would have been able to survive him. I would have ended up with nothing better to do. I'd be baking him cakes without a thanks in return. Instead of well-deserved thanks, I'd be handed contempt and a few more months in the ward. My chances of a good life would have been snuffed out. Thank God I did finally get out.

I often wonder what keeps me from going over the edge. I marvel at how far I really am from it. Most days I'm running on only a few hours of sleep, but I still manage to live a full and good life. I do amazingly well under my circumstances. I think my faith is what keeps me sane. I have a simple faith based in simple things. The little ways that God speaks to me are my reasons to stay far from the edge. Jesus gives me reasons to believe that my life, even when it's hard, is a beautiful life. They're my reasons to "Get out!" and expect more from life than what could otherwise come my way.

God speaks to me. He often speaks to me through my memories and experiences. He speaks to me simply, and beautifully, of my past. He uses it to encourage me and help me see my life as something wonderful. He speaks to help me choose something better than what life sometimes seems to be offering me.

God spoke to me, just the other day. As I sat on my parents' side porch, I reflected on how I once found shade there, in the heat of the day, when I was just a little kid. I recalled how the porch was shaded by the veranda above, as well as by big pine trees and a large sweet cherry tree. I remembered swirly iron chairs, with soft floral cushions, that made my side porch a good place to sit. I thought about how one chair bounced with you if you gently bobbed on it. I reflected on how the deer came really close to the porch when you sat there quietly and waited. The memories caused a warm feeling to wash through me. It felt like God was swimming inside me. I saw the beauty in all those simple, little, wonderful things. It all made me desire a beautiful life. It made me desire a life that was different than the life my boyfriend was offering me. When God gets close like that I want what He wants for me.

I broke up with my boyfriend. I want more. I reject my fears. I reject my fear of becoming my boyfriend's mother. I reject the idea that mental illness is what life has for me. Instead, I see the beautiful things life has for me. I see God, I feel His warmth and I want what He wants for me. I "Get out!" and it is good.

I wonder if people can see that my life is beautiful. All the good stuff in my life far outweighs the bad. I believe it's the same for all who are willing to have eyes to see the beauty. The beauty of our lives is meant to be seen and shared. It's meant for encouragement, hope and a reason to live. No matter what happens I won't stop believing and sharing the truth; it's a beautiful life.

Finding

Safe View, Age 25

I am on my way to a new doctor's office for a regular checkup. As I'm driving my concentration wanes. My thoughts spin. I plan tomorrow's math lesson in my mind. I work out all the details. Eventually my thoughts focus on the task at hand and I realize that I'm lost. I can't seem to get back on track. I keep getting lost over and over again. I sit at a traffic light. The guy in front of me is really taking his time, while I feel pressure to make it through the intersection quickly. I beep my horn but Slow Guy doesn't budge. In fact, he waits even though the light is green. It's more than I can take. I lose my temper inside the car. I start cursing, yelling and even screaming. My head is pounding and my heart is racing. I start to sweat. I realize that I'm out of control.

I have a secret life. I'm not trying to keep it a secret. It's a life that naturally just seems to keep itself quiet. No one sees me losing control at the traffic light. People don't comprehend how I lie awake all night. No one knows that I plug my nose and down shots of vodka for a few moments of rest. All my anxiety hides within me. My friends don't feel my heart pound. They don't see how my thoughts race. They don't know the truth about my life.

The truth is that I can barely keep it all together. Right now, my parents' home is a respite for me. My dad takes care of me and he takes care of my mom. Today, there's a part of me that needs to be taken care of. The stress is just too much. When I go back home I feel like I've found an escape. I sit with my mom and dad. We talk and laugh. My dad plays his music on the hi-fi. I feel like I've gone back in time. I'm a child again. I feel like I don't have to handle everything on my own. Someone is looking out for me. I feel safe.

I hold on to a good memory that makes me feel safe. It's a memory of dancing with my dad as a child. I'd stand on his shoes in the middle of our living room, wrap my arms around his belly and clasp my hands around his back. He'd lead and I'd just enjoy the ride. I think I was around five or six years old when I started to put my feet on top of his feet for a dance. When I was around 12, I outgrew dancing with my dad in this way. I was just too heavy to stand on his feet. Now, if I wanted to dance, I'd have to move my own feet to the music. That suited both of us just fine. We still danced.

I'm sitting in my living room and remembering my dances with Dad. I position myself so I can see the far side of the living room. I see the couch next to the fire place, the door with six window-panes that leads to the side porch and the hi-fi that played the records we danced to. I see everything my eyes saw when I danced with my dad in this place. We would both assume the same position each time we danced. I'd look beyond my dad to see the same comforts of home that I see right now. Today they all look back at me and urge me to remember.

I want to remember. That's why I want to paint. This is a safe view that has become connected to many of my safe and happy moments. What I see grounds me; it grounds me in a world where I often feel like I'm losing ground. I paint the safe view. I paint what my young eyes would see while I danced in the safety of my dad's arms. Those were good times and my paints make sure I don't forget.

God is so big that it's hard to picture myself being near Him. I try to remember how I've been with my own dad, and I try to transfer what I see to God. I can't do it. I just don't get how I could wrap my arms around something so vast. I have no clue how to dance with Him. Jesus is different for me. I can picture Jesus. I can see His face. I can see His eyes. I try to picture what I'd do if I could be with Jesus. I think about what I'd do if He just walked up to me and gave me the chance to touch Him and be with Him. I think I know what I'd do. I think I'd ask Him, "Would you like to dance?" I wouldn't fear that He'd say no like New Boy said no to me at my seventh grade dance. Just like my earthly dad loved to dance with me, so would Jesus. I would stand on His feet and wrap my arms around His waist. I'd let Him lead. I'd feel very safe.

I try to transfer the love I've felt with my dad. I try to transfer it to Jesus so He'll feel real to me. Sometimes I lock my bedroom door and put on some music. I stand in the middle of the room with my hands open. I close my eyes and I dance. Inside my mind I picture that the very feet of Jesus Christ are under mine and my hands are wrapped in His. I find that I feel like a child again. I find that I feel very safe. It's my favorite way to dance.

Today is not a safe day. I can see how unsafe my world has become. My good memories and good things are beginning to lose their power to bring me joy. God seems so far away. Counseling just isn't helping anymore. I can't sleep. I'm exhausted. I'm a mess. I try to hide the truth of how I feel inside. I try to prove that everything is OK, but it isn't OK. The truth is that I'm not doing very well at all. I have anxiety and it's destroying me.

I know I could come undone without some serious help, so I ask my counselor for a referral. I have my first appointment with a psychiatrist. I tell the psychiatrist that it is time for me to take medication. He didn't have to warm me up to the idea. I knew I needed it.

I have a diagnosis. I'm in the Diagnostic and Statistical Manual of Mental Disorders. My psychiatrist says I have a mild anxiety disorder. I guess, technically, that makes me "mildly" mentally ill. I have a little pink pill that I take for my anxiety. It's ironic. I was so afraid of the label that came with the medicine, but I needed it all so badly. My pink pill makes me healthier than I've ever been. Today I see just how much I need it. It's part of the truth of who I am.

I want to be a person who has it all together on her own, not someone who needs medication. I hate the label but I have to accept it along with the truth that the label reveals. It's the truth that I'm not perfect. I do have some problems. I do have an anxiety disorder and I do need the pills. They help me sleep and they stop my thoughts from spinning. It's not the answer I wanted but, oddly, it does answer my prayers. I can sleep now. I have peace. I'm finding joy again. God is right beside me.

My pink pill has a down side. It backs me into a corner. For some, it's a reason to disregard me, my feelings and my passions. In some circles, I am someone who won't be heard or acknowledged. Everything I do is seen as a manifestation of my psychiatric problem. I've lost my equal footing in exchange for escape from the pain. When I get stuck being someone's excuse, or escape from responsibility, it's really not fair. That's when my pink pill becomes a big frustration and a trap. Yet I take it. Without it I can't enjoy the beauty that surrounds me. Without it I can't rest. And without rest there is no joy. Without joy I cease to be who I am.

Simple things bring me joy. Joy matters. I want to share what matters. I don't want others to miss the vibrant colors, the warm breezes and the moments that the sunlight rests on them. I want everyone to see the beauty in colorful flowers, the simple warmth of the morning sun and the tender love of dancing dads. I want everyone to see beauty in the little things. These things matter. They are part of who we all are. Regretfully, I need my pink pill to hold on to what matters. I need it so I can push far back from the edge and begin to really share all the wonderful things around me. I'm Alisa and I love my life. I love people. I love the simple beauty of the world around me. And I have joy. This is who I am and I want to keep me. I want to share me. I want what's me to make a difference in this crazy world. That's why I take my pink pill.

Sharing Makes a Difference

I Am Pleased, Age 26

My mom and dad have always believed that common interests are the glue that holds a relationship together. They encouraged me to find a man who liked the things I liked and valued the things I valued. I imagined the perfect husband. I imagined what he would be like and the things we would share. I had a list in my mind. The list had all the things I desired in that man I would marry. It was an exhaustive list.

I found my husband, Craig, at a party in the city. We started up a conversation and I started going down my list just in case Craig could be the one. I kept checking things off of the list in my mind as he answered my questions. I got more and more excited as the conversation went on. "Check, check, check," I thought. "He's perfect."

Craig and I dated a few times before I began to see who Craig really was. I began to see that God made Craig differently. He made Craig differently than any other man I could ever meet. Craig was His plan for me. The way Craig moved and laughed, his way of being careful with me, his touch, and even the way I heard his heart pound in his chest when I held my head to it, all felt like home. Craig was made from my heart's desire.

My pink pill lets me enjoy falling in love with Craig. It also allowed me to sleep last night. I feel fantastic today, and that is very good. It's my 26th birthday. I am having the best birthday party ever. Everyone I love the most is with me. I'm surrounded by my family and my best friends. We're having a barbecue at my parent's home. It's a beautiful spring day. Craig has come

and he brought me a thoughtful present. He's nice to me and my family. I think he might really stick around. I can see my future and it looks really good. Everything is full of hope and promise. I have so many of the miracles I've prayed for. I have joy. It's joy I've never known. Today I am fully alive.

I took some pictures because this is a day I want to remember. I want to save my 26th birthday party. I want to remember the smell of the blooming lilacs, the love of family and friends, and the promises of good things to come. I use the photos to help me re-create the place where it all happened. I paint the place where the sun shined on me in all its fullness. It is where I knew for sure that God had not abandoned me nor forsaken me. I capture the light and the colors. I capture the promise. What I make resonates with hope. I am pleased.

I am pleased. My life is stuffed full of wonderful things. God is real and is really changing my life for the better. I can't keep the truth of my life quiet. My joy and enthusiasm are bubbling out from inside me. My smile sparkles. There is light in my eyes. My steps are light. I tell others about my joy. I tell them my story with the hopes that they will celebrate with me. I want to give others the hope that I now have to share.

Celebrate

Perfectly Good, Age 27

Dating Craig is wonderful. It probably wouldn't be so wonderful without my pink pill. Craig has a pace. I can keep up with his pace because I don't lie awake in the dark and meet the morning with exhaustion. Instead, I can wake up with Craig when the alarm goes off. Some days we go skiing and are on the slopes by early morning. Craig shows me how to tackle the big moguls on the double black diamond slopes. I ski faster and harder than I ever have. Each day on the slopes is an adventure. Each day with Craig is an adventure. My pink pill life can be exhilarating.

My pink pill life can also be quite passionless. Some days I sleep while the alarm keeps going off. I wake up feeling sluggish and it takes effort to push through the day. I feel dull. Dull is not who I really am. I take the pill because the options just plain suck. I don't want to feel like hell all day long. I want to sleep in Craig's arms, not lie awake in them until morning.

It is good to sleep in Craig's arms. I feel safe when I lie next to him. I let him close to me because he is the one. I was so afraid I wouldn't be capable of this kind of closeness. I think God would have preferred that I save myself for marriage. That's the way He has asked us to do things. But, I think He understands why I didn't choose to do things His way this time. I think He knows how afraid I was. Now I'm not afraid anymore. I thank God. I thank Him for giving me His best even when I was too afraid to do things His way. I thank Him for giving me Craig.

Today Craig and I are celebrating our last Christmas apart. Once we're married, we'll begin sharing the holidays with both of our families. I'll miss the way things used to be. I'll miss the barrels of ornaments coming down from the attic and the fir tree that is outside waiting. I'll miss the colored lights that are put around the kitchen window, the stockings that are placed in front of the fireplace, the mistletoe that's hung above the French doors leading to the dining room, and the green, bell-shaped music box that gets hung from the living room door knob. These are simple, little things but when Christmas is spent with Craig's family I will miss them deeply.

As a child, I was sent to bed before the final Christmas touches were put in place.

Now that I'm an adult I get to help with the very last details. My little nephews are the ones who are sleeping. We're all excited to finish decorating so we can wake the boys. We want to see their faces looking upon the fully decorated tree, and its ocean of gifts, for the first time.

We wake my nephews. They come downstairs and see it all. We delight in their delight. Then we sing. We sing even though we can't sing well. Together, we stand before the tree, fully loaded with blessings, and we sing about that silent night. We sing just one song, but it's the best song. It's a song that brings nostalgia mixed with hope that one holy night, when all was calm and unsuspecting, Jesus came. I feel indescribable peace. The fire crackles, our voices sing out of key, and I know why this night is so splendid. I am surrounded by people I love very much, and I am certain that He is real. Every other good thing I can imagine pales in comparison, and all that matters to me is joined together in one glorious moment. Love surrounds us all and is all. Life, for one moment, is perfectly good.

Jesus Christ is perfectly good. He is "Silent Night," my husband-to-be, the glory of a Christmas tree and the hope of a baby growing inside me. He is love for me. He is love for us all. He is my story, and my story to share, with whoever is willing to listen. He is what makes my life perfectly good.

Undeserved Grace, Age 27

I have dull, sluggish Pink Pill Days. I hate the way my pink pill makes me flat. I'm going to stop taking it. It will be wonderful to have my energy and enthusiasm back again, but that's not why I'm going to stop taking my medication. I'm pregnant so I have to stop taking it. I hope I'll be OK without it. I want to be able to sleep and feel good.

I'd like a healthy baby and I'd like to be a good mom who's awake and healthy too. Some of my future looks uncertain but I've decided I'm not worrying about what's going to happen down the road. Now I'm looking forward to the future. I can see baby showers, first birthdays and anniversaries. My future is full of hope.

Today is full of hope. Today is my wedding day. It is so much more than I could ever have imagined it to be. Everything is perfect. Dad has planted flowers in the gardens. Hanging pots of impatiens add color and extra charm. Life and green is everywhere. The sun is shining. The sun is shining on me.

My dress is beautiful. Everyone I love is around me. My first child is subtly growing within me. And I have a husband. He's kind, smart and funny. He's handsome. I'm no longer just a "me." I've become part of an "us." I haven't been lonely or sick for a pretty long time. Maybe I've reached the mountaintop? Maybe I'll never come down?

Jesus answered my prayers. He gave me the life I have prayed for. I have everything I've ever hoped for in a wedding day. I should be completely happy but I'm not. I push the sadness away, but it still lingers below the surface of all that preoccupies my thoughts today. I try to ignore the nagging truth; it's the truth that I'm a wimp. I actually told the minister not to use the "J" word, so I wouldn't offend my non-Christian attendees. Jesus just wasn't invited to my wedding and that leaves me full of deep regret. I have all my nostalgia, my memories, my husband, my growing baby and so much more that I've desired. I don't deserve any of it, but God is so good so He gives it all to me anyway. Jesus still gave me a wedding gift today. It was the gift of undeserved grace.

In spite of my wimpy nature and pathetic people-pleasing, nostalgia still nips at my heels, catches me and fills every moment of August 3, 1996, with warm memories and much happiness. Wimpy and groveling moves aside, it has been the wedding of my dreams. A banquet hall of incredible stature would have, by comparison, waned next to the simple beauty of my childhood home filled with family, friends and my new husband.

I conclude that my wedding day, albeit broken, is still very beautiful. Even my broken stuff is beautiful. God does that with my broken stuff. He takes even our worst moments and turns them into something worth hoping for. That's what God has done with my moments anyway. It's why I want to tell people about what I have that's worth hoping for. I want them to have what I have. I want them to have hope in both their light and their dark places. I want them to share that hope with others. Together, we might even turn this crazy, broken mess of a world into something worth hoping for.

Receiving

Beautiful World, Age 28

I'm so excited about what's happening in my life. Craig and I are moving out of our apartment and into our first house. It will have space for a nursery. It will allow room for my paintings too. I've left my teaching job. After I've raised my kids I might go back to work. It's too far off to predict for sure and I don't care to predict. I'm too happy about what's about to happen in my life right now. I can't think of anything else.

My "Womb Series" is a reflection of my connection with the life growing within me. I create differently. I'm dabbling in abstraction. I mix sand in my paints to add texture. I use vibrant colors against dark outlines. Flowing shapes fill the rectangular frame. I work quickly and boldly. With new life growing inside me I find a new way to express things. I want my art to resonate with the change that is happening in me and to me.

I'm excited to have my little girl. Yet I know that right now she is closer to Heaven than she will be again until she passes on. She's warm inside of me and she's with me all the time. She has everything she needs and knows nothing of longing or pain. Her world is perfect and I am her world. There's not much time left before Emily enters our world. For now she's safe and warm in hers. When she is born everything will change. She'll learn about joy and pain, nostalgia and words like "bittersweet." She'll discover God and love as well as isolation and hatred. She'll learn that Jesus is always with her, but she'll sometimes wonder why she's so alone. She'll learn that this beautiful world can be unkind and even dangerous. I'll do my best to help her in this life. I'll show her sunsets, flowers and oceans.

I'll teach her to remember the best times and accept the sorrow. I'll make sure she knows about God so the world will somehow make sense for her. And I'll help her create. Maybe she'd like me to teach her to paint? Then she could keep account of her own journey. Then she would have a way to mark the distance between the womb and Heaven with what matters most to her. I pray I will be able to give her this incredible gift, and I pray she will use it well. I pray that she will paint.

I want to give Emily desire even more than I desire her to paint. It's the desire to share her story that I really want to give to her. It's her story that has the real power. Painting just helps her tell it. Maybe Emily will tell her story, but she'll tell it differently than I have? Maybe she won't paint but she'll still find another way to give her story a voice? Then her life could touch people, reach out to them and encourage. That would make her life a gift for others. I'd be so incredibly proud.

Reach Out to Others

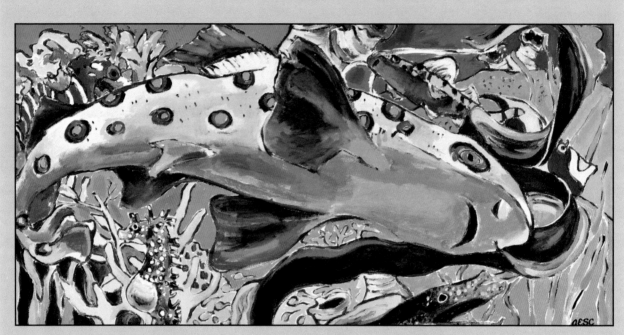

Healing Waters, Age 29

Now that I've finished nursing I've gone back on my pink pill. It makes me sleepy all the time. I feel a new kind of tired. It's different than the tired that plagues me when I don't take my meds. Without my meds I feel exhaustion. Everything hurts. My head throbs. I'm in pain. With my pink pill I'm sluggish, groggy and dull. Everything, including me, is bland. Nothing excites me but nothing hurts either.

My little "Joy" girl keeps me awake in the med's fog. Her joy is enough for both of us. I am blessed with sweetness and life. Emily is always smiling and full of enthusiasm. My mother used to say that I was her "Joy." Today, Emily is my "Joy." I want to enjoy her joy. If I could get out of this fog I'd enjoy her joy more.

Being off the medication doesn't work. It hurts too much to be awake without reprieve. I do my best to hold on to what I can still feel in my lethargy. I paint the colors and creatures of the sea because they remind me of a time when I could feel. Ocean art overtakes the walls of our home. The rooms of our house have become fanciful aquariums. What I make gives me another reason to stay awake.

As I paint, I remember tasting salty ocean water on my lips. I remember the feeling of hot, gritty sand rubbing against my chubby thighs as I built a sandcastle on the shore's edge as a child. Warm memories flood over me. My senses tingle at the thought of sand between my toes and my body bopping in the waves. It takes a lot to make my senses tingle, so I grab at the chances to feel something. My experience has been deadened by a sluggishness that's now a part of me.

I pop the pills because I must. I think I've forgotten what it's like to be fully alive, but the memory of too many sleepless nights is sharp and clear. I have so much of what I've wanted but I'm too tired to celebrate it all. The worst part is how I've lost my energy to share. I once shared my life with others but I'm too lethargic to offer it to anyone. I'm needy and clingy. I consume the hope that others have to give me but I give them nothing in return. Thank God people share their hope with me. I need what they give so badly. Today, it's the hope of the lives of others that gives me hope.

The Colors and Creatures of the Sea, Age 30

Path to Heaven, Age 31

I got pregnant again. Like with Emily, I went off my pink pill, so my baby would grow right. I felt nauseous a lot and my sleep became all messed up again. Once I was done nursing I went back on my meds. I knew medication had become a part of my life that I needed to accept. I understood that life wasn't perfect and neither was my body. I saw how my body didn't work right and never would. I saw how my pink pill was forever. I wished there was a better life for me but I knew there wasn't.

Once AJ was born we moved to Michigan. I couldn't imagine how being so far from so much of my family, and the support they gave me, would help any of us. I moved because of that "gut feeling." I knew in my gut that God wanted me to move. I paint so that I can take my old life with me to my new home in Michigan. I use my paintbrush to capture the bright colors of impatiens that surround my parents' home. I do my best to capture the beauty of these very familiar flowers and the way that they remind me of the warmth and sensitivities of my father. I decide that I will plant colorful flowers in a garden in front of my new home. I consider filling hanging pots with brightly colored flowers so I can still taste what I left behind. Considering the ways I can make myself feel at home in my new home brings me peace mixed with sadness. I realize there is no flower I can plant, or painting I can make, that will let me take it all with me. It's unavoidable. Much that I love just can't come with me.

I know what can come with me: the memories, the love and the hope life has offered me. Time and space can't steal the goodness of my past. It can't stop me from offering my life as hope to others. No matter what happens, I'm still going to share what I've got to give. No matter where I go, I'm still going to share my story.

AJ is a new part of my story. He is everything we could have wanted in a baby boy. AJ loves balls, hockey sticks, trucks and cars. He is a healthy and happy kid whose

enthusiasm for many things keeps me on the move. I have little time to think about the transition I have made from New York to Michigan. I'm nursing, unpacking and finding my way around in a new place. Some days I don't even have time to think about how sluggish I feel. The days are filled from beginning to end.

The walls of our second home are covered with the paintings that I have made so I can remember. I'm so glad that I have them now, because I can't just go to the places in my paintings whenever I'd like. My old home is far away, but my paintings let me go back whenever I'd like. They tell the story of where I've been and how I got here. And they inspire me to continue sharing my journey.

My joy-sucking meds are a part of my story once again. I wish I had my feelings back, but I lost them in exchange for the pink pill perks. I miss the joy, enthusiasm and passion I used to feel. I can't have these things anymore. If I stop taking my pink pill I'll just get sick again. I can't make it without my meds.

My new neighbor, Kathleen, thinks that I believe a lie because I believe my meds are forever. Kathleen thinks the people at her church can help heal me. I know Jesus and I've asked Him to heal me a million times. Kathleen doesn't understand that this is the way things are going to be for me. She refuses to accept it and she says so. I think she's very nice to care but I find her thinking foolish. I've known about God all my life and I understand how Jesus heals people. He doesn't heal everyone and He's made it clear that He's not going to heal me. Kathleen can't offer me the life she thinks she can, but I still have enough reasons for living: my two beautiful kids, my husband, my family and friends, my memories, the certainty of God and this beautiful world. That's enough for me.

When I sit in my hammock swing, with the sun warming me, I am offered a true reason for living. Sometimes I close my eyes and pretend that I am in God's arms and He's gently rocking me. I enjoy the motion of the swing, the idea that God might hold me, and I look at what's bursting forth from my garden as though it were put there just for me. It's my own little piece of Heaven.

I love irises. To me they're the pinnacle of garden beauty: especially the purple and white ones. After living in our new home in Michigan for the fall, winter and spring, God revealed a special surprise just for me. Purple irises were everywhere. There were more purple irises than I could transplant or give away. Hordes of purple irises surrounded our Michigan home. They grew indiscriminately and with fervor. They were just like the purple irises that would bloom in my parents' yard every year. When I see the irises I know something for sure. I know it deep down in my gut. The irises assure me that Michigan is really where I'm supposed to be. The beautiful purple, pungent flowers are God's sweet way of reminding me that I did end up where He wanted me to be all along. Irises remind me that my home is where God is, and that in the end, He will bring me back home again. Sometimes I wonder if a path, with irises on both sides, will lead me home to Heaven.

I paint the irises to tell a story. They tell the story of a girl who loves a God who gives her irises. It's a story of hope and encouragement where there should be none. The irises say, "This world can be hard, but you're never alone. God will always be with you and one day He will bring you home." I love the story that my iris picture tells. When people look at it they wonder why it was created. They ask me what the irises mean and I tell them. My iris story usually makes people smile, and sometimes they share their own story in return. We're both encouraged by what we've shared. It's another piece of Iris Heaven.

Encourage

Leaving

I'm a Believer, Age 32

I decided that it was worth considering that Kathleen could be right. Maybe my pink pill isn't forever? I mustered up some new hope for a new life, flushed my pills and stopped sleeping. It wasn't all bad. My energy and enthusiasm had returned. I had missed myself. I was glad to have me back.

Kathleen invited me to her crazy church. The church promised healing and deliverance. I knew about healing but the word "deliverance" was weird, scary and unfamiliar. Still, I wanted to believe in the promises that Kathleen's church offered me. The idea that God might have a big miracle, just for me, made me feel excited inside. It was like the excitement and anticipation I felt as a young girl holding a boy's hand for the first time. The possibility that Jesus might do something just for me made my heart ache for my own miracle. I wanted desperately to believe.

I went to Crazy Church but I was uncomfortable there. The music was really loud and repetitive. Everyone waved their hands in the air and talked in gibberish. One lady was dancing in the aisle and waving a flag in the air. People began dancing. I felt isolated and frightened. Still, the idea of a world with miracles continued to make me curious.

I quickly discovered another reason why Crazy Kathleen's church would make me uncomfortable. They didn't just believe in miracles. They believed in demons too. They also believed they could cast them out through this "deliverance" thing. I saw the idea of demons as frightening and deranged. Delivering someone from the demons seemed even more insane and scary. The last time I visited Crazy Church the whole demons thing made me want to run back home. Then I realized that if I went home my bed would be waiting for me. I didn't want to lie in it so I stayed.

After the usual arm waving, dancing and singing ended, this speaker guy came up to the podium. He started talking about this thing called our inheritance. I thought, sarcastically, "Yeah, my inheritance. It's a prolonged inability to sleep eventually leading to mental illness. Yep, that's my inheritance." Speaker Guy finished up by inviting us to participate in this thing called Prayer Ministry. It was an opportunity to have a few people pray for you so you would get, supposedly, healed and delivered. In spite of all my misgivings, I gave the Prayer Ministry a shot. I walked to the front of the church and waited my turn for prayer.

A man and a woman called me over when it was my turn to be prayed for. I found myself skeptical, yet remarkably hopeful, about what was about to take place. After I explained my prayer needs, my little team put their hands on my arms and shoulders and started to pray. The very second their hands touched my body the most intense nausea I have ever felt washed over me. The ill feeling would have brought me to my knees if I hadn't asked to be seated in the nearest pew. I left Kathleen's church thinking, "That was really weird," but expecting nothing from my Prayer Ministry encounter.

I got much more than I expected. Little changes, and big ones, began to show themselves. I used to experience feelings of dread that just weren't as intense anymore. I stopped coughing all the time and my seasonal allergies and bronchitis went away. Antibiotics became a drug of the past. I also felt a little stronger and less afraid. I still had a host of problems, but I lost many of them too. It was a big enough difference for me to be sure that God did show up that night to heal me. I also began to see that there was a "something" that affected me. I saw that it could make me sick and it wanted me to believe that I was on my way to the nuthouse.

After that night, I stuck it out. I kept going back to Crazy Kathleen's church. I also began to have new ideas about the spiritual world around me. I started to believe in evil as a distinct being with a personality and desires. I considered that evil was somewhat like God but opposite Him. Maybe evil could make me sick and make me mentally ill too? I began to see the spiritual world like a seesaw that I could exert pressure on, with God on my side and evil on the other. I saw how my thoughts and actions could make that seesaw go up or down. This was the first time I believed in an "opposition." Until then, I had no idea that I could do things to make that seesaw tip. I had learned I had the power to change spiritual things.

I always knew God was the one who really made things change. I understood that I didn't have that kind of power all by myself. When it came to "my power," people in Kathleen's church urged me to exercise it in an unfamiliar way. They urged me to expect things from God. I had never done

this before. When I prayed I was a beggar and a pleader. I groveled and I didn't expect much at all. Now I was being asked to expect health and wellness, peace and joy. It all gave me hope for change that I ached for.

I prayed and I expected. That didn't make a difference in how well I slept. I employed every strategy I was given, but things still didn't change when it came to sleeping. Some said I didn't have enough faith, or I didn't ask with enough authority, to get what I asked of God. A few considered that I had a hidden sin that stopped my prayers from working. I wasn't as excited about the new hope I had anymore. Now I was confused.

Kathleen's church confused me but it also helped make space for a new voice to speak inside my mind. In the past, I had thought and spoken garbage pretty regularly. I'd say, and believe, things like "I'm going to end up sick like my mom, I will eventually be mentally ill and Emily could end up being sick like me." Now I started praying with expectation of more and speaking of better things. The voices in my head started sounding more hopeful. Now the voices said things like, "God has a plan for me and it is good. He's going to offer me and my kids a better life than my mom and I have had. We're going to be well." It was a new voice and it made a difference.

I think God liked it that I stopped speaking garbage, but He continued to answer me in His own way and time. He wasn't about to be manipulated by me. There were plenty of people at Kathleen's church who understood that God wasn't about to be controlled by human expectations. These were the people who really helped me "get delivered." They patiently supported me on my journey. Together, we spoke of God's good plan for me, and my family, without expecting immediate or exact answers. We tried whatever we could to help me get better. They gave me much hope and support.

I had once seen my body as something I was powerless over. I had determined that what was happening to me would continue to happen and, very likely, pass itself on to my kids. Before, I saw it as my job to live as my mother had lived and to teach my kids to do the same. Like my mom's life taught me, I would not ever give up trying to live as best I could under the circumstances. I aimed to live for my kids as my mom had lived for me. I didn't have much hope for my future. I also had little hope for my kids' future.

Eventually, I began to see the danger in my thinking. I saw the danger in not fighting back. I began to understand that I wasn't exerting any pressure on the spiritual seesaw. I just sat on my side and let the forces on the other side do their thing. I sat there and expected me, my mom and my kids to be sick.

I did begin to fight back. I began to say that I was going to live a different life than I was living. Every day I exerted a little more spiritual pressure. I began to fight to tip the seesaw rather than to accept it and placate its present position. Up, down, up, down, up, down it went. I started believing that I would be well. I began to insist that my chil-

dren would live healthy, happy lives. I also started to pray and read my Bible a lot. When I was awake all night, I read my Bible and prayed until morning. I read scripture out loud as a way of grabbing for the promises that I spoke. I did it all to make the "opposition" sorry for trying to push me off the edge. It was my new way of exerting spiritual pressure. It all gave me a sense of empowerment. I had found a more hopeful way to live.

I was quiet about my thoughts on the "opposition" for quite a while. I knew that some people considered the "D" word to be a crazy person's word, so it took me a while to use it. I was afraid of becoming crazy so anything that felt crazy was hard for me to sidle up to. The Bible helped me with the "D" word. It spelled it out: DEVIL. If I believed that the Bible was true I had to face the devil on my seesaw. I had to stop sitting in the middle, canceling out my weight. I had to pick a side.

I made apologies when I used the "D" word. I didn't want to make people uncomfortable and I didn't want them to think I was crazy. That didn't work really well. I couldn't fight an enemy I wasn't willing to address. If I wanted Alisa back I knew I would have to stop being such a coward. If I wanted all of her, not just what I was but also what God intended me to be, I knew I'd need to fight the devil. It became clear that I'd need to use his name. I was also sure it wasn't God's plan for me to be sick or nuts, so I decided. I decided to be on the side with the Crazy Kathleens. Now I say the "D" word all the time. I make no apologies. I believe the devil exists and I tell him, regularly, to go to Hell.

Someone recently tried to tell me that I was crazy to believe in the devil. They tried to say I was nuts to think that the battle of good versus evil was real. I argued the opposite. I said that it was stranger to believe that the spiritual world didn't exist. I realized that I had come to truly accept the battle as the everyday, ordinary part of life. I had discovered a truth. It was the truth that "the battle" was not earth-shattering or surprisingly unique. I finally understood that ordinary lives were spent battling. I had come to know, for sure, that Crazy Kathleen had been right all along. God did have a better life for me.

I've moved away from so much of what I once believed. You can see it in my paintings. Today I paint the Battle of the Seesaw: the good, evil, demons, deliverance, angels, miracles, battles, Heaven, Hell, hope, seesaws, the devil, God, Jesus, crazy, sane and all the rest. I'm a believer.

I want others to move with me. I want them to be believers. I tell everyone I meet about the Battle because I know it's real. People need to know the Battle can be fought and won. The seesaw is part of my story and I share it to bring hope and freedom to others. I also encourage others to share the truth. It's the truth that God can help us win the Battle and lead us to an even better life than the one we already have.

I'm a Believer, Age 32

My Cup Overflows, Age 32

I planted this incredible backyard garden during our first summer in Michigan. The soil behind our house was unbelievably fertile. Vegetables, pumpkins, sunflowers, zinnias and strawberries burst forth from the ground with zeal. It was my one and only "Green Thumb Summer." God had blessed everything in and around our new home including the soil for my new gardening hobby. I put whirligigs, scarecrows and playful garden ornaments throughout the rows of edible and colorful things I had planted. The sunflowers were gigantic and the pumpkins got big enough for carving in October. Everything thrived in my new garden.

Unlike my garden, I'm withering. I'm still struggling to make it without my meds. Without my pink pill it's hard to thrive. What choice do I have? I've made the only choice that has any promise of hope. I'm trading my flatlined, boring and passionless self in, so I can get my old life back. It's a life of sleepless nights, headaches and anxiety but my passions and enthusiasms have returned to me. The meds made me feel like I was swimming in tar. The devil loved that. He wanted me slow and listless, so I wouldn't have the energy to find a life of fullness and joy. I have to get myself back no matter how much it hurts. The way I've been living has become a dead end. I've been sleepwalking. I've been in a coma. The devil wants my life to be lived his way. He'd like me to be either passionless or crazy. I'm fighting against him for a good life full of joy.

I don't want my children to accept suffering like I once did. I want them to expect something different. That's why I refuse to be dull and lifeless and I refuse to go crazy. I'm not just fighting for myself. I'm fighting for my kids. They'll expect to live as I have lived. I'm the one who shows them what to expect and how to get it. This is how I'm going to make fertile soil for my children and grandchildren. I'm going to show them how to expect a harvest that's rich and full. I'm going to teach them how to reap a life of joy.

Right now I'm in the middle of a fight for a good life. My head hurts, my body aches and my thoughts are weighed down from exhaustion. I still refuse to believe that Jesus can't do something for me. He's not powerless. I'm not going to let my kids see me live for a God who is impotent. I refuse to settle.

Who am I? What have I done to deserve a life with promise? I paint my garden. It's overflowing. It's teeming with life and hope. My garden is a picture of what can be for me. I also paint the chocolate cake my old boyfriend's mother gave him. It's a picture of what could have been for me. It's a picture of what could have been if I became the next cake maker. It's a picture of a woman with no hope. I paint what is and what might have been. What I paint recalls how God reached in to my life and plucked me from what could have been. It marks the day that I began realizing how much better life could be.

A memory reminds me of what could have been for me. I recall having judged a woman who was preoccupied while her children played in the nearby playground. I concluded that a good mother would watch her children all the time so they'd always be safe. I think back to a recent time when my kids were at the lake with me. I struggled to keep my eyes open. I was incredibly tired, and I fought to stay alert while AJ and Emily played in the sand on the lakeshore. For just a minute I slipped away. I was lucky it was just a minute and not five or ten. If it had been longer I might have found my face plastered across the five o'clock news screen with the words MOTHER ABANDONS DROWNING CHILDREN AT LAKE AND TAKES A NAP. I see that I'm worse than that preoccupied mother. I'm way more like the mother who abandons her children than I'd like to admit. I have a good life that I don't deserve. I've forgotten to give out grace when I have been given it

so freely. I haven't earned my rich gardens teeming with life and joy. I don't deserve God, what He has given me and all He has promised me. Yet my cup overflows.

I share because my cup overflows. The stories of my life are the overflow of goodness, joy and undeserved blessings I have known. I can't help but share them. They are my chance to show others the blessings that might have otherwise been forgotten, lost or missed. Sharing is a chance to offer others the hope that's right there with them. It's an opportunity to encourage people to offer others the same hope that's been offered them. I believe we've all got a story and we've all got a little hope to give. We all have the overflow. We all have something to share.

We All Have Something to Share

Worth the Fight, Age 32

I think I've actually met evil. I'm not talking about your regular, run-of-the-mill thief or liar. I'm talking about the real thing: a twisted individual, completely disturbed and hurtful in their actions, with no capacity whatsoever for remorse, introspection or personal responsibility. I'm talking about someone who is totally untouched by someone else's suffering and who takes great enjoyment in the misery, pain and suffering of others. In fact, they delight in it and do their best to bring about the darkness in everything with their twisted, sick thinking and behavior.

In one case, the evil I faced was very close to me and everyone I loved was just working around it. No one called a spade a spade. No one spoke the words, "She is evil." Instead, they excused the person on the premise of mental illness and instability. To me, it was very clear that the individual knew exactly what she was doing. When Gerald and I were little, she'd toss coins onto the floor, in the middle of the room, and tell us to fight for them. She'd laugh and enjoy watching us push each other and grab at each other's share. Over time this woman had somehow managed to lose her soul. Her humanness and her essence were completely given over. There was, I am certain, something unnatural operating in this person's body and mind. The individual was way beyond sick. In fact, the person who once was in her skin slipped away over time. The light went out in her eyes. She was just a shell and inside it lived darkness. What was left was wicked.

This person's funeral marked one of the saddest days of my life. Until this day, I had never been to a funeral that left me considering the possibility that the person went to Hell. Hell scares me. I try not to think about it especially when it comes to imagining that someone might be rotting away there for eternity. I pretty much figure that we'll all have a big party in Heaven. I imagine all the messed-up, selfish, difficult people like me will be there as well as your occasional saint. I believe Jesus loves everyone and His forgiveness is beyond our imagination. He's everyone's backstage Heavenly entry since we've all blown it and messed up many things on earth.

We can usually find threads of goodness even in the most hardened and difficult people. These threads are usually shared at funerals as a way of redeeming the life that was lived. At this funeral there was no thread. Nothing was said. There was not one good thing that could be remembered of this person. I'd known her for over 30 years so I tried to think of a time, or place, where I'd seen some gentleness or kindness from her. Everything I could recall was demented and twisted. The church was stale and cold. It felt like death in there. There was no taste of a life restored.

To make the funeral even sadder, people joined her. Two lives sold out that day. They used this death to benefit their own selfish souls and their own already overstuffed pockets. It was horrible. Thank God they're not dead yet. There's still time for their U-turn: their turn from darkness and towards the light. I imagine the day when they've changed and I can hug them and feel safe with them. I pray that they'll make a U-turn. I've been told that U-turns are hard to make when you've been going in the wrong direction for a long time. They say that the current sweeps you along and picks up pace. Evil seeks you out. It waits until it can grab you and pull you downstream. It looks for a weak moment and then it makes you weaker. God has to reach into your life and pluck you from the darkness if you are ever to get away again. You can't make the U-Turn on your own. At this point, moving towards the light is like turning a tanker ship. The pressure and energy that must be exerted in order to begin going in the right direction is enormous. The movement from the darkness and into the light is monstrous. Success can't be found in your own power. The battle, at this point, is much, much bigger than you.

I try to imagine what the battle must look like so I can put it on my canvas. I know that my own battle is much, much bigger than me. That's why it is so hard to win. I make a painting that shows what I see when I imagine my battle. I make a dark side and a light side. I include the weapons of warfare from the book of Ephesians. They are the things that I use to fight when the battle has become much bigger than me. They're the tools God has given me to use when we battle together. The sword of the Spirit, helmet of salvation and the breastplate of righteousness are in the forefront of my canvas. The devil winds himself around a tree in the background while tempting others to taste his ungodly fruit. There are angels and evil in my painting. The angels sing of the gospel of peace with the belt of truth buckled around their waists. I put evil on the dark side and make a bull's-eye that is scanning the light for an opportunity to get someone in its range. I know the devil catches people in his bull's-eye, much like the two people who sold out at the horrible funeral. I know that after he finds them, he lays bait and pounces the very moment they give in. Now only God can get them back, but He doesn't do it alone. We battle with Him. In my painting I am battling with Him. I imagine that my life, and even the lives of those who have sold out, can be redeemed.

The trees that surround the frame of this painting have meaning. They are miracle trees from a miracle walk I took with a wonderful friend. God came into the woods with us and lit up the tree tops as though they were on fire. All around us were magnificent trees with glowing embers for branches. I believe that everyone in the woods that day, even those who were refusing to know Him, imagined that God was real as they looked up into the glowing sky. I suspect someone made a U-turn that day, so I include a U-turn symbol in my composition. I think someone might have made their U-turn because God reached into their world and made magnificent trees with glowing ember branches. The miracle trees make my painting because they show the power of God. It's the power that U-turns are made of.

After seeing miracle trees Wonderful Friend and I saw a miracle sky. It was split in two by a beam of light. The light rose from the horizon and shot up towards the heavens as far as our eyes could see. We just stared. It was the most unusual sky I have ever seen. Miracle Sky reminds me that my God can split the sky in two. He is my safe place and my shelter from the enemy. The devil scans the horizon but he can't find me because my God rules the sky. He tells the heavens what to do and they listen. I add the miracle sky to my canvas. The sky's glowing beam splits my painting in two. It separates the light from the darkness. It shows the power God has to change any life.

My painting reminds me of all the miracle trees and miracle skies of my life. I remember all the incredible moments when God reached into my ordinary life and did something extraordinary for me or someone else. I remember meeting Craig, my miracle prayer team, the respite pink pill, Crazy Kathleen, friends and family who love me, sicknesses healed, hearts softened, marriages mended and the beauty of purple irises. I remember the deer in my parents' backyard, one rose in a vase, a tiny glass cup of little white and yellow crocuses and dancing with my dad. I recall holding my mom's hand on the way to the Strawberry Place, playing on the sandy shore with Gerald, trips to the ocean with my friend Maureen and eating potato chips with my older brother. I imagine my big sister's magic canvas bag, Emily's joyous giggling and nursing AJ with his sweet, warm body cuddled up to mine. My painting reminds me of all the reasons why the battle is worth the fight. God has loved me. God loves me now. The proof is part of me and all around me. My canvas holds the reasons why I will never stop fighting for the life God has promised me and others. It holds all the reasons for sharing my story.

Worth the Fight, Age 32

Luckiest Mother Alive, Age 33

I watched a television program about prisoners of war. One way to torture them was to constantly interrupt their sleep. Once they'd drift off they'd get poked, probed and prodded. Eventually they'd start to go nuts. I'm just like a POW. On the bad nights, POW's get more sleep than me. I could go nuts. If I go nuts I'll join the marginalized. I'm pretty afraid of being marginalized. In some circles I've already been marginalized; I'm not taken seriously, I don't have a say and I'm treated in a condescending manner. I fill out a health questionnaire in the doctor's office, and I mark off the box that asks if there's a history of bipolar disorder in my family. I mark off the box because it's the truth about someone else. The box is about them, not me. My doctor is abrupt as he enters the exam room. He greets me with a superior attitude. He enters the room with his mind already made up. I tell him about my sleeping problem and he offers me meds for bipolar disorder. I tell him that I'm not depressed and I'm not manic. He looks at me like I'm too stupid to know what's happening to my own body. I couldn't get this guy to listen to me if I tried. The script was in his hand and he hadn't even met me yet. He saw the box I checked off before he even met me, and then he marginalized me.

I want to belong and I want to be understood. I want people to value me and enjoy me. Being marginalized is the antithesis of what I want. I notice people who don't belong and I find myself understanding them. I feel connected to them because people do the same things to them that they do to me.

I saw a girl about 19 years old in the supermarket with a small baby. It looked like she didn't have very much money, because the car seat her infant was in was dated and worn. The girl wore a dirty T-shirt with a front pocket that was filled by a box of cigarettes. In her cart was some no-brand peanut butter, bargain basement diapers, baby formula and a bottle of cheap wine. There was no wedding band on her finger. When her baby cried the girl didn't respond. Instead, she wandered the aisles looking aimlessly. People stared at the girl. Some showed disgust and made comments under their breath. I have to admit that I stared too. My first inclination was to judge this girl. Her baby was crying and she wasn't taking care of it. The baby started screaming and there was still no response from Mom. This mom looked like a poster mom for child neglect. I marginalized her. She wasn't a person. She was a beast.

I had another response. It came second. I imagined what it must be like to be a 19-year-old mother who was broke, husbandless, overwhelmed, cold and exhausted. I considered that she might not have a car. Then she would need to lug her groceries home in the snow while dragging her baby alongside her. I wondered what it felt like to be so young and with so much responsibility. Maybe she had no resources and no one to support her? I made eye contact with her and I smiled. She smiled back at me through weary eyes. She wasn't a beast. She was a young girl who was all alone. The people in the supermarket pushed her away. I know what it feels like to be pushed away.

Being marginalized is scary because you don't usually get grace. Instead, you get judged. I can't honestly tell you what I'd do for my screaming baby if I was 19 and alone. Maybe what this girl did was neglect but it was also human. When a person is marginalized you'll find people around them who've forgotten what the truth is about being human: people need support, understanding and a place to belong.

I love my church, because grace is given out handsomely. My church friends know all about my fears, my pink pill, psychologists, struggles and weaknesses. I'm still invited to join in and help others. I'm seen as someone with a strong spirit and determination. I'm not marginalized. Instead, I'm given opportunities to rise above my circumstances. My church challenges me to be something greater than the world says that I am. I'm trusted and affirmed.

I hate being marginalized. If I end up with bipolar disorder I'll be marginalized even more. Some people who know my label will define me by it. Like it was for the girl in the supermarket, people will draw conclusions about every move I make. They'll look in my cart and make judgments about what they find there. If they find wine they'll decide I'm self-medicating. If I'm talkative they'll see manic. If I'm offended, they'll see oversensitive. If I'm tired they'll see depressed. Everything will be skewed by what they know and what they think they know.

I finish the last of three paintings about my fears. I add the words "Lord, teach me to risk." The words of my painting weave through some of the scary places I know and have known. As I paint, I consider what's scary for me today. Mostly, I'm scared about what people will think. That's why I'm afraid to be seen as bipolar, mentally ill or anxious. It's also why I fear the condescending words and judgmental thoughts of others. I'm trapped in fear because I try to control something I can't control: what other people will do, think or say.

I'm afraid of the places where I won't belong. I work really hard to please people and make things seem a certain way, so I'll belong everywhere at all times. I need to trust that God has a place where I belong, and believe I don't have to work so hard at pleasing people anymore. I need to forfeit my attempts to control. I need to risk trusting Him.

I dream about horrible things. They're all things I fear and can't control. I dream of tornadoes and atomic bombs. Sleeping is Hell. I hate the darkness.

In my last tornado dream AJ was surrounded by a swirling tornado of danger and I had no control. I awoke to remember some fearful moments I still can't quite shake. I remember having drawn a bath for AJ. He slipped into the tub, fully clothed, as I folded laundry in the next room. I heard the splash, ran and pulled him out. Just a few days later, AJ fell out of the shopping cart. The hood of his parka broke his fall so he wasn't hurt. I felt incompetent, like a mother who couldn't keep her child safe.

I paint Emily's tender hands wrapped around AJ and I revel in the thought that they will love and protect each other. Still, behind them loom the atomic bombs and funnel clouds of my dreams. I show the bathtub water that AJ slipped and fell in. In the bottom left-hand corner I paint a dark, dank crawl space from my parents' basement. It's a space I feared greatly as a child. I add good stuff too: some pumpkins from my miracle garden, swirly wrought-iron furniture from the gazebo with a thousand windows, and some rosary beads that belonged to Aunt Julie are mixed in with the chaos. I wonder about the reality behind the painting I've created. I wonder if the good stuff or the bad stuff is more powerful. At night, I realize, is when the bad stuff creeps in. When I'm alone and exhausted in the dark is when the bad stuff gains power.

Emily and AJ are at the center of the painting because they are my center. I paint them in their Halloween costumes. Emily is dressed like a fairy and her warm arms surround my little son's body. I remember making Emily's fairy costume. The piece de résistance was a crown of twisted pastel-colored tulle with a train. Emily was delighted with her costume. AJ was equally enthused wearing a fuzzy, zip-up suit that had a hood with big donkey ears. When I put it on him, he became the cutest little creature I had ever seen.

Halloween was on a beautiful fall day that year. The sun was bright and crisp and the sky was clear blue. I put the kids in their costumes so we could go outside and take pictures. I had two rolls of film to shoot that afternoon and it simply wasn't enough. There was just no way to capture how in-nocent and sweet my kids looked to me that day, but I wanted to try. Emily danced around with her wings as though she knew she was beyond beautiful. AJ ran around the yard bursting with enthusiasm and anticipation. When I ran out of film I just stood there, watched them and loved them. I felt like the luckiest mother alive.

That Halloween is imprinted in my memory. That day my life was good and I knew it. All the reasons to love my life ran around and danced before me. Emily and AJ were, and are, my center. They are the reason why, even at night, the good stuff is still more powerful. They are the reason I refuse to let the bad stuff take over. I fight for my kids. They're why I'm not going to let the bad stuff win.

I won't let the bad stuff win. That's why I won't stop sharing the good stuff. That's how I make sure it has more power than the bad. When I paint I include the bad stuff but it never wins. When I share my paintings I also share the stories within them. They are an impetus for offering the stories of my life as hope to others. They're also an impetus for others to share their story. A simple vignette from my canvas can open a conversation of mutual encouragement and much-needed support. In the end the pictures I make are inconsequential. It's the sharing of lives that makes the real difference.

The Best I Have to Give Her, Age 34

When I was about eight years old I spent my summer at the Field Club. Most of my memories of the Nyack Field Club are nostalgic and wonderful. Everything was really good there. At least, everything was good as long as I was careful to avoid the benches.

At the foot of the bathroom stairs were several long benches. Sometimes the benches were empty. Then I could sigh in relief and pop up the stairs to the bathroom. Other times the big kids were sitting there. Sometimes big kids are nice to little kids and sometimes they're not. This group of big kids made sport of teasing and tormenting anyone younger or different than them. When the benches were occupied, I avoided them with fervor. Eventually, I would have to "go" and I'd be stuck facing the Bench Beasts.

One day I forgot to be wary of The Beasts. I had found a butterfly with beautiful wings. At least, one of them was beautiful. The other wing was half missing. I didn't care. My butterfly was beautiful and I was excited. Full of enthusiasm, I went to pass the benches with the hope of making it to the restroom quickly. My mom had just come off the court, so I had a good chance of meeting her in the bathroom. When I found her I could show her my beautiful butterfly. Cut off at the pass, I was delayed by an older girl at the benches. "Watcha got there?" she asked.

Shocked that she seemed to be interested, and with total innocence, I presented my beautiful, but maimed, treasure to the inquirer. "It's a butterfly!" I said.

"It's missing a wing," she balked. "Did you eat it?"

"No, I didn't eat it," I stammered.

"Yes, you did," the older girl taunted. "You ate the butterfly's wing." She began to sing: "You're the girl who ate the butterfly's wing. You're the girl who ate the butterfly's wing." I tried to pass her but she wouldn't let me through. I tried to turn around and go the other way but she followed me. All the while she mocked me with her vicious song: "The girl who ate the butterfly's wing. You're the girl who ate the butterfly's wing." Tears welled up in my eyes and spilled out. She was not moved to pity me. My pain was her amusement.

It felt like forever before I finally got away from the taunting. Once free, I began a hopeful search for the comfort of my mom. Reaching the front of the grounds I looked out to see I was too late. Her trip to the bathroom over, my mom had resumed her tennis game. Kids were forbidden to approach adults while on the courts. Hope of a hug and some protection from the Bench Beasts was gone. I found myself a bench away from everyone and cried while I held my butterfly prize. Sitting there, I began to wish I had never found it. The voices inside my head took over. "Alisa, you're so stupid. You actually believed she was interested in your dumb butterfly? You're a moron. Dumb fool. Fat stupid pig." The Bench Beasts, while gone, still had their way of getting at me. Finally, I shut up the voices, dried my own tears and got up. "Have fun," I thought. "Avoid the Bench Beasts." It was business as usual.

I want to protect my daughter from the likes of the Bench Beasts. I know how vicious we girls can be when we have pain inside. The greater the hurt the more nasty we become. Sometimes hurting others seems to satiate the beast inside us for a time. The world is full of broken little girls who are Bench Beasts. Some of us are adults on the outside, but inside we're the emotional age of eight. Angry and bitter, we look for a target for releasing our rage. We have good reason to be in pain. Someone hurt us. Some other little girl had pain and she passed it on to us. Maybe she found a little girl with a butterfly at the foot of the bathroom stairs when her own pain became unbearable. Girls in pain pass the pain on. My little girl isn't broken yet. She has yet to receive pain from a child in pain. I do my best to keep it that way. I keep my eyes open. I pause and peek to see where Emily is and what's happening around her. I make sure she's safe as best I can. I protect her heart whenever possible.

I want Emily to keep her innocence. I don't want her to learn that trusting is foolish. I want her to marvel in little discoveries like the beauty of a butterfly's wings. I want to be there if the Bench Beasts do come around. Then I can say, "Leave her alone! She's just an innocent little kid. Stop passing on the pain. I'm sorry you're hurting but go! Pick on someone your own size, you beast!" If I'm lucky enough to be around to protect her when the Bench Beasts come, then Emily can keep her innocence for a little while longer. She can skip up the stairs and say, "Mommy, look what I found! It's a butterfly Isn't it beautiful?"

Then I will have the good fortune to respond, "Oh, Emily! How wonderful! What a fantastic butterfly you've found."

"Can I keep it?" she might ask.

"Yes, of course. Let's take it home and keep it," could be my song. It could replace the song of the Bench Beasts. This is how I can stop the broken hearts from stealing Emily's tender heart. This is how the voices in her head will speak of love, joy and happiness rather than stupid, moron and fool.

I paint my sweet Emmy Lou as she sleeps. She looks so incredibly innocent. Her skin is creamy like a peach and her golden hair curls tightly to her sleepy head. Behind her resting eyelids are beautiful blue eyes. Her chubby, cherub-like little body is just like mine was when I was a little girl. She is perfect and safe. I also add some things to my canvas that I fear. I add the things I fear will find my sweet Emmy Lou. Innocence Snatchers swirl around the space where she sleeps so peacefully. The world is too big. So much can go wrong. I can't always be there when the Innocence Snatchers come. "Jesus, keep her safe," I pray. "Keep my Emmy Lou safe from pain, tears and innocence lost."

There was a silver lining for me after I met the Bench Beasts. I had the sense that eventually I would not be alone. Eventually I'd meet up with my mom and relate my upsetting story of my upsetting day. She'd listen and say, "Oh, my poor little Looby Loo," and offer an extra long hug. Maybe that's why the Bench Beasts didn't make me one of them. Maybe it's because I had a mom who could help fix my broken heart. Today I offer Emily the same silver lining. I know the Innocence Snatchers will come. Sometimes I won't be there when they do. I offer the promise to listen, and give her a hug, even if it comes a little too late. It was the best my mom could do, and it was enough for me. So it will be for my Emmy Lou too.

I wish I could give Emily more. Instead, I must release her heart to God. Only He can be with her all of the time. His quiet and loving voice can console her pain, dry her tears and shield her from the Bench Beasts. Sometimes, though, even He will allow Emily to see the ways our broken world, and our broken hearts, fall short of His perfect plan. I want to stop "sometimes"

from coming but I know that's wrong. I have to let Emily enter this imperfect world on God's terms, not mine. All I can do is love her, and hold her when I can, just like my mom did for me. That has got to be enough. It's all I have. It's the best I have to give her.

I'd love to offer people a story of happiness that didn't include the realities of a broken world. That's not my story. What I have to give is the story of a broken world, a broken heart and the reality of pain mixed with the ever-present existence of a loving God. I can't offer others any more than I can offer Emily. All that my story really promises is the promise of God. It's the best I have to give.

We All Have a Story

Sky Full of Angels, Age 34

I can't sleep in bed with Craig anymore. His every move and breath awakens me. That's why I now sleep on a mat on the floor. I'm awake more at night than I've ever been, so I try to do things to help me sleep better. I run a lot with the hopes that I'll exhaust myself and sleep. Sometimes I try running eight or nine miles at a time. That doesn't usually help me sleep but I feel better while I'm running.

As I run I imagine angels swarming above my parents' home. I see hordes of them keeping vigil on the rooftop. In my mind I construct a beam of light that comes down from the sky and pierces the darkness that surrounds their home. I imagine the power of whatever is dark being destroyed by the brightness. I see my angels singing a song of victory because my mom is well and my dad is dancing with her. Their faces smile brilliantly. Both my mom and dad believe in Jesus Christ. Heaven opens up to welcome them home. I play this scenario over and over in my mind. It's one of my favorite fantasies.

I like to think that angels surround the people who need them. My mom needs lots of angels because she is really sick. She's not getting better. In fact, she's getting worse. Her body has started to tremor and it hurts a lot. She's in pain and there's no solution. I pray that my mom will be surrounded by God's angels and they will set things right in her life; that one day my mom's body and mind will be whole and feel no pain.

I've made angels on a new canvas and I love them. I especially love the ones with the big, colorful wings. They give me hope that things will make sense someday. Hope that there can be a good ending for the bad stuff. Hope that there's a point to what is happening to me and those I love.

I share my angels and my stories of angels. All around me are paintings of angels. When people enter my home they see all the angels and they ask about them. It's a chance to tell others about the hope that I have. It's a chance for others to receive some hope from me and share some of their hope too. When we share, life is more than darkness. We see the light. We understand. Hope surrounds us.

Surround Someone with Hope

Darkness and Light, Age 35

Today my life is dark and light. The light is my kids, my husband, all my family, my good friends and the love of others. They are reason enough to fight for my sanity.

God has given me more light to stay the course. It came as an unexpected gift. He gave me my church. I didn't understand what a gift it was at first. Again and again time reveals the light that my church is for me. In my low places my church has been a powerful source of hope. The people there see me with God's eyes. A lot of the time it feels like they see the opposite of what I see in me. When I see weakness they see strength. When I see fear they see courage. When I see instability they see confidence. When I struggled they didn't quietly remove me from the scene. Instead, they called me out to be something more than I already was. Fully knowing the challenges and difficulties of my life, they spoke of my giftedness, insight and potential. When I saw darkness creeping in they saw greatness. They saw light. They spoke of promise and potential when I saw nothing. They've been like angels.

The Bible says the least will become the greatest. The world pushes back on this truth with lies. Adolf Hitler had a place for the mentally ill. They were first in line for extermination. They needed to be the first to go to purify the race. He would have put me near the front of the line. He would have seen me through the world's eyes. He would have seen the lies. Without people to speak truth to the places I most feared, I would have believed the lies. I would have become the lies.

I had this vision of a puzzle with missing pieces. I saw myself finding the pieces, one at a time, till I seized what God had for me. I believe in that vision. That's why I have begun a journey to look for those pieces. I met a doctor who saw something different in me. When she saw the boxes that I checked on the patient information form she didn't marginalize me. She prescribed a plan instead of pills. She helped me find a missing piece.

Part of my new doctor's plan was a sleep study. I spent the night at Garden City Hospital, and I woke up 54 times in five hours. Each time I woke my airway had closed, stopping my breathing. For the first time my crazy dreams, headaches and exhaustion made so much sense. I get a script for a CPAP machine, and it brings some relief. It helps me sleep and breathe better. I have a new piece of my puzzle. I am more hopeful today. I want more of the right answers and that's what I have. I will search and I will find them so I can be well.

I make a painting of darkness and light. The angels in my painting compete with the darkness. They're winning. Scary cellar stairs, spiders, dark, dank crawl spaces, and some other scary things I've known fill the darkness of my canvas. Some places are so dark you can't even see what's hiding there. Some places should be dark but they're not. The light exposes them and strips them of their power. You notice what's dark, but you can't miss the angels that surround the darkness. The angels are like cutouts with hard edges that contrast with the blackness. They're like the puzzle pieces from my vision.

I like them. I like my angel pieces. They remind me that I'm seizing what God has for me. One day I'll get all the pieces. I'm going to finish this journey. I will collect all the pieces. I'll collect them one God-given piece at a time.

Betty helps me find pieces. Betty is my friend. She's also my spiritual mentor. I see her for some spiritual direction. The last time we met, Betty gave me some direction. She told me I was God's Beloved and she gave me a book about how much God loves me. I can't imagine how God could love me like that. I know in my head that God loves me, but my heart has other things to say. That's why I've been thinking about how I really feel about me. I'm discovering that I'm pretty hard on myself. I don't think I'm such a great mother, wife or person. I feel like I'm always a mess and I'm always overwhelmed. I think about what I see when I picture myself. Words come to mind: anxious, uptight, irritated failure. I see how badly I want to be a better mother and a better person. I realize I don't like what I see when I look at myself.

I keep a journal. Inside it I've started writing down my conversations with God. I've always had voices in my head. One of the voices is encouraging. I used to call that voice my "gut" or "my voice." Now I know that this voice is God's voice. I put God's words in parentheses when I'm journaling. The parentheses let me go back in my journal and think about what I've heard God say. What God says is different from what I say when I look at myself. God says things like "You are My Beloved." I'd never like myself like that. That's how I know the voice is God, not me.

My latest entry was made after reading a psalm. It was Psalm 139, verse 1, and it reads, "O Lord, you have searched me and you know me." I wrote about this verse because I "know me" and I don't like me that much. I've been told that God really likes me. I struggle with the encouraging voices I hear. What if they're not God? What if they're my own fantasies or imaginations? I see how I don't like the idea that God searches me and "knows me," because I've been searching myself. I'm finding that I think I suck a lot of the time. I figure my take on the idea of being searched by God might warrant a conversation with Him. Maybe He can straighten me out? That's why I get out my journal and my pen, and I get ready to use my parentheses.

Dear God,

I don't just want to accept it on faith. I want to believe, deep within myself, that You find me lovable. I want to know that You love me for sure. I want to believe that my sins don't make me who I am. When I look at me I see STRUGGLE. I see a desperate, confused, sinful woman who is somehow managing to worm her way into a little Christlikeness. I get the salvation thing. I know that all my bad stuff is forgiven. I know I don't take it with me when I die. I understand that I'm going to Heaven, but I'll be perfect there. It will be easy to love me then. This is different than that. You KNOW me. Do You like what you see? **(I don't see the sin, Alisa. Jesus took care of that. I can't see what has already been taken care of.)** Help me, Lord. Help me to see me through Your eyes. That's how I will know, really know, that You love me. That's when I will believe that I really am Your Beloved. **(I see you trying too hard to get something you don't have to earn. Relax, and know that you are loved. I see you, My creation, and it is very good.)** Let me trust You. Let me hear Your voice and believe. **(You are My Beloved.)** Help me stop arguing with You. You know who I am. Help me to accept how You see me. Help me to believe in what You see. Let me trust Your voice.

Your Child,
Alisa

I add a dream I have about AJ to my journal. It's another dream about wanting to protect him. I think about what triggered the dream: my feelings about me as a mother. I saw a mother who wasn't protecting her son like she should. I saw someone very far from being God's beloved. I recall the time that AJ fell out of the shopping cart. I figured he was OK because I was lucky, not because I had kept him safe. I imagined that a good mother would NEVER forget to snap her child into the shopping cart seat.

I worry more about AJ now because I'm pregnant again. I want to barf all the time, so it's really hard to give him the most basic stuff like a bath or clean pj's. I can't give AJ the attention he deserves right now. I can't take my meds when I'm pregnant. That means I can't sleep to get the rest I need. I can't get the nausea to wane. Some days, doing my best to keep AJ safe is the best I can do. I knew that having another child would press my limits, but I had no idea that it would happen this soon. Our new baby isn't even born yet and I'm already coming undone. I'm trying so hard to do everything right and I'm falling pathetically short. I'm just not enough. With the birth of our third child it will be even more obvious that I am not enough. With only one of me, and three of them, it's impossible to manage all sources of harm. It's a miracle that I've managed to protect them for as long as I have. They're not safe and well because I'm a good mother. They're safe and well because I am blessed.

I keep hearing God inside my head. He keeps saying, "I see you trying too hard to get something you don't have to earn." I think that means He blesses me, and my kids, because He loves us, not because we loved enough or worked hard enough. Maybe what I need to work at is loving myself? God says He loves me. If I'm good enough for Him, maybe I should find a way to like what I see when I look at myself. Maybe I'd be a better mother, wife and person if I gave myself the grace God has already extended to me? Maybe I can't really love other people well until I figure out how to love myself?

God gives us good things because He is good. It's the truth. I am blessed and I know it. I want to make sure other people know that they're blessed too. Maybe we'd all be better people if we understood the grace God has already given us? I share my story with the hopes that we'll all come to see how very blessed we all are.

Unforgivable Sin, Age 35

Zachary was born on February 10, 2004. Zachary means "God has remembered." Zachary's warm, wet, newborn body slid into my arms along with a confidence that his little life had an important purpose. I understood that his life was not a mistake. He was too wonderful to be a mistake. I had confidence that God would not forget His promises. He would remember them.

Most days I still have faith that God does not forget His promises. Yet on the bad days I still wonder if I have made a terrible mistake. On bad days it feels like I may have pushed my limits too far. Before Zachy I had some time to take care of me. I take care of him now. He cries all the time. He cries when I'm in the shower, he cries when I move the laundry from the washer to the dryer and he cries when I use the bathroom. When he's not crying he's screaming. The only way to stop the noise is to nurse him. I sit on the couch and nurse him for hours while everything around me falls apart. I feel incredibly guilty when I let Zachy cry. I feel guilty if I try to fold the laundry or brush my teeth because he won't stop crying when he's not in my arms. I've stopped taking regular showers and I use the bathroom as little as possible. Everything around me competes with the crying. If I pick something else over the crying I feel like a selfish mother. I can't keep up with all the demands I've put on myself and all the demands around me. Right now everything feels like it has become too much.

Everything was way too much the other day. I exited the house for the pediatrician's office with two plans that I wanted to carry out: get Zachy what he needed at the doctor and take AJ to McDonald's for a special lunch. The trip to the pediatrician's went well and Zachy actually fell asleep in his car seat before we even left the office. I snapped the car seat into place and drove the three of us to McDonald's. AJ and I got out of the car, ordered our food and sat down to eat it. As I bit into my second fry I realized it. I FORGOT ZACHY IN THE CAR! I grabbed AJ and abandoned our food to get my abandoned child. Zachy slept through it all. He was no worse for the wear. As for me, I was overwhelmed by my present potential to do accidental harm.

I've never taken a really hard look at what I think of myself. Zachary has changed that. Right now, everything in my life is clearly far from perfect, including me. Beneath the surface, I can see that I am a person who really doesn't like herself if she's anything less than perfect. I know how I see myself is not healthy. I know I have to change what I see when I see me.

I'm upset about what happened with Zachy at McDonald's. I'm doing my best to believe that I don't have to be the perfect mother. I continue to judge myself pretty harshly. I come by it rightly. I live in a world where people are judged harshly. The dad who forgets his child in the car in the supermarket lot gets judged harshly. You hear about it because the father *really* forgot; it wasn't just for five minutes on the fry line. If it makes the news, the forgetting probably happened on a sweltering day. We see newscasters portray this kind of forgetful father as a selfish beast. He could be a selfish beast, but he might not be, too.

There are other possibilities.

I think we forget to ask, "Was it too much?" We think we know what motivates someone who forgets their child in the car in the middle of the hot summer. We forget that Forgetting Dad's wife might have served him divorce papers that morning. We forget that he might have come from the pediatrician's office where he learned that his older daughter has leukemia. The size of the "too much" is often proportional to the size of the misdeed. My "too much" was just big enough to make me forget for just a few moments. If things get worse my "too much" will grow.

I can't shake the feeling that I've been very selfish. How can I meet everyone's needs now? Forget being Perfect Mom. Now I feel like I'll be lucky to manage to keep my three kids alive. I don't get how God could love me right now. If He does, I think He might have very low expectations.

When I was a kid I promised myself that I would be a certain kind of mother. I vowed to succeed as a mom in all the places where I had been failed. I had this vision of the kind of mom I would be. The mom in my vision was sweet, kind and patient. She was generous with her time, playful and fun-loving. She was healthy too. I've now done many of the things I vowed I would never do. All of my expectations of myself, wrapped up with all of my failures, add up to why I don't like what I see when I see me.

Every morning I wake up and I try harder than I did the day before. I try harder to be a good mom. Being a good mom is almost impossible now. I've become too sick to meet all my expectations. When I sleep my dreams are distorted, and when I wake I'm so sick I can barely get out of bed. I'm nauseous without reprieve. Without my pink pill my CPAP is rendered useless. I suffocate in my sleep, my body jerks awake and my heart races. I don't want to close my eyes when I lie down at night. The thought makes me panic. I'm a mess.

I fear failing as a mom but I have another even bigger fear. I fear insanity more than I ever have. I'm afraid things have become way too much for me. The idea of going someplace where I will get taken care of is appealing and utterly terrifying at the same time. My kids aside, pride is all I have left to motivate me. I fight my way back from the edge because I don't want to be labeled or institutionalized. I'm still invested in what other people think about me. It's a big reason why I fear insanity. I'm driven by the opinions of others. It's pathetic.

Insanity seems like a plausible reality. I've reached a point that nothing I try makes enough of a difference. There's no escape that I can see and no hope that I can feel. I feel abandoned by everyone, including God. I raged at God last night. "You're impotent," I cried. "How long do I have to wait for Your healing? How many years must I wait for You to do something? When are You going to fix me, so I can be the person I want to be? When are You going to fix me, so I can be the person You made me to be? Are You really listening? Do You really care?" I cursed Him, too. It was absolutely blasphemous, but it was honest. I said all the things you imagine saying when you're beyond angry. I said them, just like this, in my journal:

"SCREW YOU. YOUR GOD DAMN PROMISES ARE RETURNING VOID ON ME. I HATE YOU FOR ALL YOUR FALSE HOPE. WHAT KIND OF SICK TRICK IS THIS? WHEN THE HELL DO I GET TO SLEEP? I HAVE DONE EVERYTHING AND TRIED EVERYTHING TO BE WELL. I'M SUPPOSED TO BE BETTER OFF WITH JESUS? I'VE YET TO SEE HIM COME. WHEN IS HE GOING TO SHOW UP ON THAT WHITE HORSE? DO YOU EVEN EXIST? DO YOU EVEN HAVE ANY POWER ON THIS LOUSY EARTH? ALL I WANT IS TO BE ABLE TO SLEEP AND FEEL NORMAL. ENOUGH! ENOUGH!"

I consider some terrible things. They are terrible things that I've done. They're terrible things that could happen, that have happened or that I could cause to happen. I look back over scary stuff that has left great fear in my heart. I make a painting about my fears of going mad. I make a painting about my fears of getting worse, not better. I add playing cards to my canvas. They speak of how my life feels like a series of random events in the hands of chance. Everything feels like a crapshoot. I add some angels, but I'm not sure I believe in them anymore. My painting shows how confused and messed up I am inside. It's no wonder that I'm falling short and falling apart.

I realize that I'm very afraid. I don't know where God has gone, and I'm not sure He makes a difference anymore. I think God might have left me, and I can't blame Him for leaving. I've cursed and raged at Him. I wouldn't like me after what I've done. I can't blame Him if He doesn't like me anymore. I'm not any better of a person than I was last year or 10 years ago. In fact, I might be a worse person. I think I've committed blasphemy. I've cursed God and I think that might be an unforgivable sin. I also don't feel any better. I'm in terrible pain. I'm so tired I can't think clearly. There is no tolerable cure for me. My body hurts. It's dark. The world sleeps peacefully without me. God really might have left me. I feel very alone. I think I might deserve to be alone.

"Can I still talk to God?" I wonder. I realize that I can't remember a time when I haven't talked to Him. He's been my internal voice all my life. "Without Him who am I?" I realize I really don't know how to live without Him.

I sit in the dark for a very long time. I miss God. I want to talk to Him again even if He doesn't give me what I ask for. I see that I've been talking to Him so I can get something. "Can I love Him in the loony bin?" I wonder. "Can I love Him if He lets me go there? Will I love Him if He leaves me as I am? Can I love Him if He doesn't answer my prayers?" I want to. My time in the dark leaves me with one more question for God. I'm afraid of what His answer will be but I ask the question: "I've cursed and raged at You. Do You still love me?"

"More than ever," He whispers to me quietly. "More than ever."

"I'm sorry," I say. "I'm sorry for what I said. I'm sorry for the way I said it."

I hear His voice of grace. It speaks loudly and clearly: "I already knew, Alisa. I know everything that goes on inside of you. You can't hide anything from Me. I know all your anger and your pain. I love you anyway."

I realize what I've been doing. I come clean: "I've used You. I've used You to get what I want. I've resented You for not answering my prayers. I've tried to get You to make me perfect when only You are perfect. I've tried to become You, Lord, and I tried to make You make it happen. I've tried to manipulate You, and I've cursed You for not letting me do it. Please forgive me."

"That's what I came for," He says to me. "That's what I came for."

Since my blasphemous night I no longer expect a happy ending. Danger and disturbance hide in every corner of my canvas, but God is present in even its darkest parts. I am beginning to trust God with everything He sends my way. If my prayers aren't answered I accept His will. I'll trust Him if I'm not healed and whole on this earth. I'll trust Him with my children's lives. I'll give him the ordinary moments of my days. I'll trust Him if I'm locked away. I'll continue to trust Him even if I continue to distrust what I see in me. I'll trust Him with my whole life. He's my closest friend in the joy, anger, disappointment, and in the pain.

Jesus really is my closest friend. He's such a good friend that I want to share Him. When I introduce Jesus to others, I use whatever I can to show them how incredible He is. I tell stories of how my Friend has always been with me through the ups and downs of life. I make sure I tell stories that let others know that my Friend is their Friend too. I am careful to be sure that everything I make and share tells the truth: through the good stuff, and through the disappointment and the pain, Jesus is our closest friend. I tell others about Jesus with the hopes that they'll want to know Him too. I offer my life with the hopes that Jesus will become someone else's life to offer.

Introduce Others

Etched In Her Hands, Age 36

My CPAP machine is just one piece. I have reentered the world of pink pills and psychiatrists to grapple for some more pieces of my puzzle. My journey is a long way from being finished. My puzzle is far from complete.

The doctors continually try, and fail, at finding the right pieces for me. Fewer and fewer options remain with each failed attempt. Medications for narcolepsy, seizures, ADHD and anxiety are on a long list of supposed solutions. When solutions fail, I lose some more hope. I'm beginning to approach the edge: the end of the line. My dad had to watch my mom reach the end of the line. It was the place where my parents chose the lesser of two evils: medication with horrible, life-sucking side effects over insanity. It was a very sad place. It was a place where hope died.

I refuse to let hope die. While unfinished, my puzzle frightens me and causes me, and others, pain. Still, God is with me. He's helping me find all my pieces. He makes sure they're the right pieces. He has real wisdom and true answers. My puzzle will not make a picture of hopelessness when all the pieces snap together. God won't give me pieces that don't fit with the vision He's given me to seize. Jesus will make sure that not one piece is left missing when my last day is done. This is the hope that I can pass on to others who need some hope: one day we will all be exactly as we're supposed to be. We all have a shot at becoming who we really are.

Zachy just turned six months old and has begun to take more than a catnap here and there. I can make a little art while he's snoozing. It helps me show how I'm becoming who God intends me to be; I'm less quick to judge, slower to hate, more at peace with who I am and more accepting of the way things are. Each piece I create marks these shifts inside me. Each creation shows how I'm another step closer to what God intends me to be.

How I see myself is shifting. I see my perfectionism. I see how it makes me expect too much from myself and from others. What I'm discovering is helping me make the shift. I'm making a shift from disliking myself to accepting myself. I'm changing my own expectations so they include grace for me and others. I'm beginning to see how God gives us grace and how He desires us to receive it. I'm changing my expectations so they look more like God's desires. These shifts are huge shifts for me. They're happening because I'm learning to trust the "gut" voice inside of me. I'm also learning to trust who the voice is; it's not me at all. The voice is God and it speaks truth. God says, "You're not a bad mother, Alisa. You're not a selfish person. I don't believe that you are a failure. You don't deserve to be alone. I'm proud of you. I'm proud of the ways you're willing to change and grow. Start believing the truth of who you are in Me. Don't try to earn My love. Don't use Me to try and become a perfect person. Instead, accept My grace and trust that I love you just as you are. Also, trust My eyes. I like what I see."

Journaling is really driving "The Shift." It helps me hear what God says. When I write to God, He writes back. Sometimes

He just writes to me. I put His words down. His words put goose bumps on my arms. I feel like God is right with me as I journal. I feel like He's moving my pen and my heart all at the same time. What God and I are doing in my journal is changing me. It's a good shift. I like it. God likes it too. He told me so. He told me in my journal:

My dear Alisa,

(Alisa, my sweet child, I see your struggling. I hear your cries. It's OK to fall short. You can't possibly meet the world's expectations or yours. But you can meet Mine.) What are your expectations? **(I expect that you learn to love yourself. I expect that you learn to love Me and others even more. All I want from you is that you be willing. Are you willing to try to learn these things?)** Yes. **(That's why you please Me. You're willing.)** Anything else? **(Keep talking with Me. Keep writing. And remember how much I love you.)**

With pleasure,
God

I desire to be willing. I want to keep on shifting. I want to give more grace to myself and others. It would be great to give great forgiveness to the people around me and to myself, too. I'd like to judge less, and lower my expectations, so that the people I know can be more perfectly loved by me. I so desire to hold on to what's beautiful to me. Maybe what God is teaching me will help me see even more beauty in the world. I'd like that. I hear God's voice. He says, "I'd like that too."

There is beauty in the world. I know this is true even in the most difficult places. My life is proof that beauty is at work in everyone and everything: even in the most hardened people and places. I share my life to encourage others to see the beauty and share it too. Sharing allows all of us to help keep the beauty alive.

I boldly share the most beautiful truth of my life. It's the truth that I'm a Christian. I believe that Jesus Christ is God's Son. I believe our salvation can only be found through Him. I don't think I'm better because I believe these things. We all understand some truth but it's in bits and pieces. I know that Christians carry foolishness and lies. So do non-Christians. We all have our idols that we worship. We all have our lies we believe. We all have ways we fail to love. We can't hide the things that we store in our hearts from Him. He knows all and He still loves us. That is the beauty of the truth.

I pray for all of us. I pray simply. I say, "Jesus, don't let us miss You. Let us know who You are. Let us want You more than life itself." I pray we will all, no matter what we've missed along the way, know the truth of who He is. I pray He will take us all home.

I make a new painting. I use torn papers, feathers, glitter and ink. I fill a huge canvas with a big angel with huge hands. I imagine that her hands take my prayers up to Heaven. All the people that I pray for have their names etched in her hands. My name is in her hands too. I need my name in her hands just as much as all the other names need to be there. I believe what the Bible says about salvation and getting to Heaven. I also know that I'm way too stupid, flawed and selfish to meet the requirements for perfection. I need a Savior just as much as the next guy.

If you know me then know it's true. I pray for you. Your name is permanently etched in my angel's hands. I believe that Jesus is the Savior of your world and mine. I believe He's the real gig and I pray you will believe it too. Don't be offended. If you don't believe please don't be offended. I don't think I'm better than you. Spinning around in my head, and in my soul, is so much rancid garbage. My prayer is the best thing I have to offer you. It's my simple prayer that we'll all recognize The Beautiful Truth. I pray we will all recognize Him when our day is done.

Next to Jesus on the cross was a man who was a horrible thief and murderer. He lived his life missing it. He didn't get the gig. Yet in his last moments he understood. He looked at Jesus and knew who He was. He also wanted Him. His heart desired Jesus and that's all that was required. His murderous acts were washed away. He went to Heaven that very day. I pray we will all die like the thief. I pray we'll all die knowing and desiring Him regardless of what we've been, believed or done.

I want us all to die knowing and desiring Him. I believe my life is proof that Jesus is worth knowing and desiring so I offer it. I pray that others will accept the encouragement I have to give them; Jesus is truly worth knowing and desiring. He's the greatest encouragement all our lives have got to give.

Give the Greatest Encouragement

Your Mother's Daughter, Age 37

I have a new psychiatrist through my bargain basement insurance carrier. I get this sinking feeling that I'm not getting the help I need from him. I need a really good psychiatrist. Meanwhile, New Psychiatrist just keeps trying different possible solutions like he's pulling them randomly from some errant pile of possibilities. He gives me a diagnosis of ADHD along with a script for speed. Then he tacks on a prognostication. He says, "If this doesn't work (the speed) you might want to consider that you might be your mother's daughter." I wanted to pummel the guy. I wondered if he slept through Psychiatry 101. I was pretty sure his words were on the "Top 10 Things You Should Never Say to Your Psychiatric Patient" list.

Somehow New Psychiatrist managed to find the perfect words and actions to match my deepest fears. He sent me home with a prescription for a stimulant as well as a list of different drugs for me to research. He told me I should do my research right away since any reaction I might have to the stimulant could be immediate. The drugs he had on that list were all for bipolar disorder. They were all the drugs my mom had taken: the drugs that couldn't stop her disease and gave her a painful, incurable, degenerative movement disorder. He said I should decide which of those drugs I'd like to take next since the stimulant could likely cause a full-blown manic episode within the next day or so. Even though I'd never had a manic episode, this guy half expected me to exhibit all the symptoms of my mom's disease within the next day. I drove home wondering how I was going to switch from being ADHD to bipolar in just 24 hours. I thought about what life would be like for my kids if their mom walked around looking like a mental patient. When I got home I sobbed in Craig's arms. At that moment there was no point I had known that was lower. I had reached my personal bottom.

The stimulants don't cause me an episode of mania and I begin to sleep a bit better. At the same time I feel really edgy and irritated. Over time New Psychiatrist raises the dose again and again. Each time we raise the dose I give the meds time to work. With each tweak I wonder if I will finally satisfy New Psychiatrist's presumptions: his bipolar prognostication. Eventually, I find myself on the maximum dose. I don't feel right. My stomach is always wrenching and my heart races. I feel pain in my chest. I tell New Psychiatrist that I feel wrong inside. He switches me to a drug for narcolepsy. It's a stimulant too. I'm beginning to wonder if you can be driven to bipolar even if you weren't bipolar at the start. I also wonder if New Psychiatrist would notice if I stopped scheduling my appointments. I'm in his office once every three months for 15 minutes. It doesn't seem like enough supervision over a woman who he suspects could have a manic episode overnight. I'm pretty sure I'm not getting the care I need. Unfortunately, I've reached a point where I need the best care I've ever had.

The stimulants make things worse over time. In New Psychiatrist's defense, there's no knowing in advance what the side effects will be. There's also no knowing what medications will even help. It's all guesswork. A voice in my head speaks to my fears: "Pick a card, any card, Alisa. It's all a gamble. You're in the hands of chance. God isn't watching. He doesn't care. Your doctor isn't paying attention either. No one gives a crap. You're on your own." I try to embrace each new adjustment. I allow time to test each change. It's endless trial and error, and some of the trials frighten me. I'm also sicker than when I first stepped into New Psychiatrist's office.

Would you have a biopsy if there was no tumor? Would you go through radiation treatments if they didn't find you had any cancer? I don't fit the diagnostic criteria for so many things that I've been told I have or have been treated for. Doctors enter the room with the bipolar checklist or the checklist for depression. I'm honest when I check off the boxes that describe me. I tell the truth when I don't mark a box. Some doctors give me looks that suggest that I'm lying or denying the truth. They don't understand that I'd do anything to meet the diagnostic criteria that match their suspicions. Then I'd have an answer and a solution to try. Then we might find a treatment that would work for me. Then I could be well. Today I'd settle for the pink pill if it would bring me some relief, but it doesn't work for me anymore. I'm feeling more like I'm in the hands of chance than I ever have. Yet I still believe in God. The voice in my head that says He doesn't care is lying. I fight the lies that try to tip my seesaw towards the dark side. God's angels are all around me. They surround me and embrace me. They fight for me. With them there's always hope.

I use my journal to write a prayer of hope. I send the prayer up to Jesus instead of to God. That's new for me. Jesus has a face in my mind. I can see Jesus and that helps me pray. I imagine that I could touch Jesus if He showed Himself to me. He once walked the earth and felt the earth beneath His feet, just like me. When I pray to Jesus, I know He understands how I feel. Just the idea of being understood by Him gives me hope. Right now hope is mostly a decision, not a feeling. I'm trying to accept the way things are and trust that Jesus has a good plan for me. I can't really do all the things in the prayer yet, but I say it all as I believe it will be done in time. I just send the prayer out to Jesus and hope that He answers it. With Him there's always hope.

Dear Jesus,

I know my journey is not supposed to be about what You can do for me. I'm always praying for You to heal, fix or change me. I know that You are not just about making miracles. If You were, I'd be healed, fixed and changed. Instead, I think You're more about relationship. It's about my relationship with You, isn't it? **(Loving you, and bringing you to understand how much I love you, is the greatest gift life on this earth can offer you. Our relationship is life.)** I can't get away from Your love. You're always there, even in the really dark places that I find myself in right now. I accept that You have a purpose for my dark places. I accept them, yet I resist them too. I resist what I can change and accept what I cannot. When it all seems so incredibly meaningless, I will remember that You, Jesus, are my friend. I will remember that

Your love carries me. And I will remember that true freedom lies in my eternal life with You. I know that today is full of exercises that will prepare me for a richer relationship with You. It's all in Your hands and it's all part of Your good plan. So, with no strings attached, with no expectations and with no demands, I pledge my love and devotion to You. I pledge to trust You, and embrace my relationship with You, no matter where it takes me.

You are the outcome that I'm really after. Forgive me for my anger and foolishness. I have used You and I have loved You for what You could do for me. I don't want to use You anymore. I want to know You, and if suffering is part of that then I embrace it. With one foot in suffering, and the other in the abundant joy and peace I know from being in relationship with You, I commit my life to totally and completely pursuing You. With reckless and foolish abandon, I accept the senselessness of this world: its pain, wickedness and torment. I also accept the joy and peace of seeing You everywhere and every day. I cling to my relationship with You, for it is the only true way to have joy and peace in this crazy life. Forgive me, Jesus, for demanding that You fix everything. I don't want You to fix everything anymore. Instead, do whatever it takes for me to know You more. Jesus, You are what I seek. You are my hope in this life.

Your child,
Alisa

Ready for Heaven, Age 37

I want to be ready for Heaven when I die. I want Jesus to be proud of me. When I'm suspicious of people or I think the worst of them, I realize how poorly I love. I know that the word "love" is used a lot in the Bible because Jesus wants us to work on how we love. Mostly, I do love people, but sometimes they really get under my skin. That's when I realize how NOT ready I am for Heaven. Last night I asked Jesus, "How will I ever be ready?" He answered me:

Dear Jesus,

How will I ever be ready? **(You won't be on your own. I'll take care of your weaknesses. I'll make you ready.)** I haven't prepared myself. I'm not ready. **(Your whole life is preparation. The ebb and flow of human weakness, and My power manifested in that weakness, are part of the up and down of the life everyone lives. That tension will always be there. One day, you will feel confident, connected and full of life. The next, you may wonder how I could possibly love you. Those are the days that you learn: the down days. That's when you learn the truth of My love. It's the truth that My love burns strong and steady even as you fail. I am your restoration. You couldn't make Me stop loving you, Alisa. You're just not that powerful and your sin isn't either. My love is the one thing you will always have. Everything on earth will one day pass away, but I will remain and so will My love for you. You are learning that My love is enough for you. I allowed your struggles. They showed you that when you had nothing left to live for, I was enough. I filled** you with My strength and I carried you. Our relationship was enough to endure what was dark and empty in your life. I became your light in the darkness. You knew My love then. You know it now.)** I don't want to just accept Your love. I want to give it to others. **(It's one and the same, Alisa. The more you accept My love, the more love you have to give away. One can't be without the other.)** So I just let You love me and believe that You love me? That's all I have to do to love others better? **(That's it for now!)** Thanks. **(No problem!)**

Gratefully,
Alisa

Mostly, I really do love people. People are my angels. There are so many people to love, and so many people love me in return. Every time I put an angel on my canvas I'm reminded of the people who are angels in my life. Today I make a new angel. She has golden wings and shiny blue hair. Her purple dress is loaded with stars. I make the sky behind her a shiny, deep, blood red and I fill it with shining golden stars. I decide I couldn't make her more beautiful. I'm happy when I look at her.

I think about the things that make me happy. The way I love my kids makes me happy. I love helping them grow and learn. I love loving them. I love watching Emily's latest performance. I love watching AJ defend the goal. I love holding Zachy in my arms after his bath. I hold him in my arms and cuddle his clean, sweet-smelling little body.

I love my family. They know things about me that I don't even know. They laugh with me, not at me. I love how they love me for who I am. It's love without conditions. It's just about the best love I know on this earth.

My friends believe I can do just about anything. I have become things I never expected because of the ways they call me out to be more than I believe I am. I had no idea how much my friends would stick with me. I had no idea how much they'd be willing to do for me or be for me. How they see me is light.

I love creating. I love painting my hopes and dreams. I love making something that's beautiful to me. I love making something that shows who I am inside and what I feel. I love sharing what I create with people and watching how my creations bring them joy and encouragement. I love sharing my story with others. It's like giving a little piece of me to someone wonderful. It's one of my favorite ways to love the people who have loved me. It's a way I can be an angel in return.

Denying

People I Can Count On, Age 37

Lynne is one of my angels. She met up with me after church the other day. While she talked to me I felt like I had stuck a wet finger in an electrical socket. The morning of teaching Sunday school had overwhelmed me. I looked over my pile of Sunday school leftovers. Amidst my laundry baskets loaded with supplies, and duffel bags of games and equipment, swirled my three children. What sat before me was the aftermath of one too many good things all being accomplished on stimulants and two weeks without sleeping. I told Lynne how undone I was feeling. Lynne then loved me with the words of an angel.

Lynne started talking to me about living life in this thing she called The Spectrum: the bipolar spectrum. She kindly and carefully suggested that I might have a place in that spectrum. She didn't mean it in a bad way. In fact, she talked about my creativity and how it was one of the gifts of living in The Spectrum. Lynne recommended a book that I might read about creativity and people like me. Her ideas sounded plausible, so I was willing to look into them.

Till this point I never considered the idea that, while I might not be bipolar, I could still be going up and down in little ways. When Lynne spoke I imagined a scale of one to ten. I pictured a really bipolar person as a nine or a ten and a really depressed person as a one or a two. Then I asked myself where I thought I fell on the scale. I knew I wasn't a five. I could see I was mostly a six and sometimes a seven. A few times I might have even approached an eight. The idea that I was bipolar didn't make sense to me, but the idea that I might be a six or a seven in The Spectrum did. The concept was strangely relieving.

I thought about how I was feeling inside as Lynne spoke. I didn't feel good inside. The stimulants made it easier for Lynne to explain The Spectrum. I didn't feel right because of them. The stimulants were forcing me to figure out what was going wrong inside of me. I read the book Lynne recommended and I was comforted by it. It talked about the gift of going up and down in little ways. I knew these "little ways" described what happened inside of me. The book described my smaller vacillations as an opportunity to make the best of the creativity and insight that comes with The Spectrum. I considered that being in The Spectrum, in the way that I was, could be a good thing. I realized the opportunity of being not quite bipolar. I wasn't going up and down in the bigger ways that rob people of the gifts of The Spectrum. Little vacillations allowed me creative abilities and insights that I could tap into and exercise. For the first time, I considered that I might not be as sick as I had thought. Properly managed, maybe The Spectrum was a gift, instead of being a curse to fear?

As I looked at the remains of my morning ambitions I knew what I needed. I had to find a way to grab hold of the ups and downs and rein them in. I also had to find a way to get off the stimulants. They were driving me towards becoming a nine or a ten. A doctor who could help me find a way back from the edge was a necessity. A psychiatrist who was invested in helping me was irreplaceable. Much of what I was doing to help myself needed to change.

So much was happening to me that I needed God's help to change. I had all these pieces, but I didn't know how to fit them together. I couldn't make sense out of The Spectrum, sleep apnea, narcolepsy, ADHD, my fears and all the other things that were, could or might be a part of me. I kept thinking two words: I'm done. I told Jesus, "I'm done." Everyone who really knows me had heard me speak the words, "I'm done." I was done because I'd reached out for help and I'd gotten worse. I was also done because I just was. For some reason I couldn't bear it all anymore. Being awake all night made me sick and then I'd be sick all day long. I'd really met with the darkest place I'd ever known. This place was way worse than some of the places I'd been. Those places were bad, but this place was really the bottom. Everything felt like death. I wondered if my life was worth living.

I was the tanker ship that needed a new direction. What was required to turn me around was massive. I desperately needed a U-turn. I knew I needed Jesus to make it happen. I had a new journal. I flipped to a fresh, new page and I used it to ask Jesus for some much-needed encouragement and new direction. As always, He was faithful to provide it.

Dear sweet Alisa,

(Who do you need, Alisa? If I heal you in every way you won't need Me anymore. You'll just go on NOT needing Me and doing everything for yourself. What do you want to believe? Do you want to believe the lie that you can have everything you want and be perfect on your own?

Or do you want to understand the truth that you don't have what it takes without Me? Your world is coming undone, Alisa. You need Me. Only I am enough.) I need You. I do need You. Without you I really am done. **(When you realize your need for Me, I can come with My peace and My restoration. You're done if you keep trying to live by your own power. Now that you realize how "done" you are without me, I really have permission to give you what you've needed all along. You're not "done," Alisa, you're not going to die, and you're not going to lose your mind. You're going to live and you're going to live in peace. You're going to live in Me and I am going to live in you.)** That's how You do it, isn't it? That's how You defeat the evil and sinfulness in this life. You use my sin, and the sin of others, to turn our hearts towards You. You use the darkness that lives on this earth. You use it all to make us realize how much we need You. **(That's how I turn darkness into light, Alisa. I work redemption in the hard places. I fill the holes that sin makes with My love. I tricked him. The devil thought he would bring destruction to you. He cursed you. He wanted you to die or lose your mind. That was his plan. Little did he suspect that I would redeem you through his curse. In Me, sin has no power over you, your mother, Emily, AJ, Zachy or Craig. My forgiveness, grace and love will overpower what would otherwise destroy you and your family. Piece by piece you will give Me control and I will put you back together. I'll put the people around you back together too. I'll do it through Me inside of you. You're not "done,"**

Alisa. I have every piece you need. Real life, through Me, is just beginning.)

**All the hope you need,
Jesus**

I'm grateful for my new journal and the way God talks to me in it. I'm also grateful for a book I'm recently rediscovering. It's a book on codependency. The book is all about being a people pleaser, caring about what other people think and being a slave to other people's wants, needs and opinions. It's a book all about me. It's about many of the reasons why I've believed "I'm done." It's the voice of God just for me.

Exploring codependency helps me understand why some of my relationships are suffering. I had expectations. I expected people to love me as I had loved them. I expected people to meet me in this terrible place I have found myself. I start to change my expectations. I let people meet me where they can. I let them be where they are when they're with me. I try to have compassion and I struggle to forgive their limitations. I try not to hold others responsible for my needs. I try not to be codependent.

Loving people requires loving those who don't always love you back. That's real love instead of codependent love. Right now I'm having a hard time loving. It's not easy to love people who can't come beside you. There are people in my life who are quick to tell me how to behave. They're people who think they know how to behave so they tell others what to do, think and feel. They think they're perfect so they tell everyone else how to be perfect for them. It's

difficult to love Perfect People when your own life is so far from perfect. I feel like I'm entitled to more. I feel like I deserve to be loved back. I'm angry that I'm not. I see how wrong that is. I see how codependent I have become.

I reflect on how Jesus got the opposite of what He deserved. We measured Him for much less than He was. It wasn't humanly possible for Him to take loving us so far. He didn't even keep His own body in the end. He had only a few people who were willing to see glimmers of who He really was. Mostly, He enraged people. He was a problem to be solved. He was an irritation and an inconvenience. I have such a small taste of what He received and I still can't figure out how to love. Codependents think that fixing people is loving people. We think everyone else is the problem. All our energy goes into changing other people so we don't have to look at ourselves. Everyone else isn't the problem. I've got the problem. It's a problem that lives inside my heart; it's hate. God wants to help me to fix myself on the inside. I'm going to let Him help me.

Today, my story is simple. I see how small I am and how little I have to give. It's a gritty, messy and often humiliating story. I've been stripped of every big dream or expectation I've ever had for myself or my life. I'm nothing, but I still share. You'd think that today my story has no power but that's not true. People are comforted and encouraged by the story of my life. They're comforted by the stories of God's presence in my most unexpected, ordinary and difficult places. Because their story is much like mine, they start to share too. God reaches us at the bottom of it all.

Pick a Card, Any Card, Age 38

I joined a codependency support group. It's a good place for me to be, because I need someplace where I can be honest without having to worry about what other people think. There's a rule at the support group table: what's said at the table stays at the table. That means I can tell my group "I'm done." I'm able to admit that I've lost hope. I can also tell them that I'm afraid I'm going to end up mentally ill. The words, "I might have a nervous breakdown," can be spoken. At the table I won't be judged, marginalized or spoken about behind my back. It's one of the few places where my codependency doesn't have power over me.

I'm desperately waiting for an appointment with a new therapist. I can see I'm headed for trouble. Something is really different. I don't see hope like I used to. I know people love me and I love them, too. I have three wonderful children, a loving husband, caring family and kind friends. I want to love all these good people as best I can. That's why I don't want them to watch me unravel. Maybe they'd all be better off without me? Some days it feels like we're all in the hands of chance rather than in the hands of God. I've started painting a lot more because it helps me hold on to some lingering hope. On the bad days my canvas reminds me that God doesn't play the wheel. Creating is an escape from the confusion and the pain.

As I create I think about many people. I think about people who have been wonderful to me. They are so much of what's good and right in my life. God, I love people. When the roulette wheel is spinning, and I don't know where the needle might land, they're my lifeline. I need people. I need people who really know how to love. I can see that my life is full of so many wonderful, loving people. Today I paint angels wearing roulette wheel dresses. I paint to give voice to some particularly disturbing possibilities. They're all random and undesirable. My angels speak. They say, "Pick a card, any card." They don't give me answers. My real-life, living angels are the ones who give me answers. They're all the people I love. They're all the people who have loved me. When the chips are down they don't fold. In my crazy, random world they have become my royal flush. They're the very best hand I've been dealt, and it's a hand I've decided that I'm willing to bet my life on. They are, when all else fails, my hope. They are God's voice when I can't hear Him anymore.

Be an Angel

Big Hit Grief, Age 38

I remember back to when my dad built us a large sandbox in the backyard. It sat just outside the edge of the woods beyond the apple trees. I was usually left alone in the sandbox unless my brother made sport of chucking green crab apples at me. The apple attack was really no big deal. There was no danger of getting hurt. The apples were simply peace robbers. When I was enjoying my private world at the edge of the woods the apples would sometimes find me. I liked my private world. I hated the invasions.

I add green crab apples to my canvas because of what they represent today. Each apple I add to my canvas is an invader of my quiet, private world. My apple angels block the attack. In the distance I add real invaders: three dark figures that loom. They can hit. They can hurt.

The three figures in my painting are from a vision that my mom had in the hospital. She was just a girl when she had the vision. My mom had been badly burned in an accident and spent three months in a hospital bed under a sterilization tent. During that time she saw three dark figures at the foot of her bed. The vision happened when my mom was particularly weak, hurting and close to losing her life. I used to think the figures could have been angels, but I don't think that anymore. If God had sent them they would have been magnificent and they would have helped her. Instead, they were dark and faceless. They offered nothing except some remote feeling that she wasn't going to die. I can't imagine a visit from three of God's angels offering so little to a little girl with a raw, charred body.

On one of my apples I write the word "grief." I have found that grief doesn't come with life's little green apple attacks. Grief comes with the big hits from the darkness. They come out of nowhere. Big hit grief is my mother having to be sick and hurting in a hospital bed, for such a long time, when she was so young. Like a little kid playing quietly in the sandbox, we don't always anticipate the coming invasion. My mom took a lot of hits. She did nothing to deserve them. That's part of why they cause so much grief. Grief is pain that makes no sense. We don't ask for it. We don't expect it. We don't deserve it. She didn't deserve it.

I've taken a lot of hits. I meet New Therapist. I tell him, "I'm done. I can't hold it all together anymore. Something needs to change." I can't handle even one more crab apple on my pile. Everything feels like too much to manage. It's all pain that makes no sense. It's all grief.

I tell others that I'm filled with grief. I let people know how everything is "too much." I thought the truth of my life would pull people down but it doesn't. People who are struggling are comforted to know that they're not alone. What I share opens up the hearts of those who need hope. We encourage each other. Sometimes our saddest stories bring the most power to touch the lives of others. It's ironic. It's amazing. It's why we share.

Touch a Life

Resenting

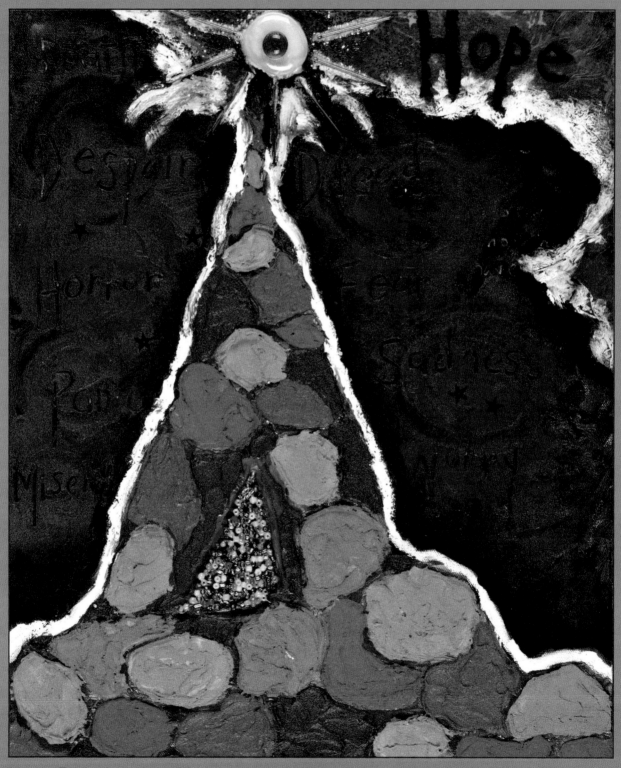

Hope Remains, Age 38

I have a nightmare. I remember bits and pieces of this horrible dream. I remember a frightening mass of rocks that's surrounded by thick clouds of horrid darkness. As I wake, I recognize my mountain of fear. It's built of all the things I can't control. I want to protect the people I love. I want the world we live in to be safe and true. The more I feel like I'm slipping, the more I see how I can't make a difference in it all. I want my life to give people hope. I'm not sure it will anymore. I don't want the people I love to see me live a hopeless life that makes them sad. If I keep getting worse, my life will make them sad. Human beings need sleep and I'm just not getting enough. Without some sleep I will have a nervous breakdown. People who have nervous breakdowns go to the psychiatric hospital. I don't want my kids to have to visit me in the psychiatric hospital. I don't hold out hope that the psychiatric hospital will make a difference either. I doubt they'll have doctors there who have more insight than the ones I've already sought help from. I haven't been a person who won't reach out for help and take it. If I had hope that the loony bin would make a difference, I'd sign myself in. That's why I wonder if it's a good idea if I keep on living. People might have to watch me waste away. I could spare them the burden by bowing out.

I ask God, "Why? What's the point of sticking around?" He tells me that my life matters regardless of what happens. He tells me not to be afraid of the scary places. He tells me that He can use me wherever, and however, He chooses. He says, "Alisa, don't be afraid of where I will send you. Wherever you go, and whatever happens, I'm going to use you. Your life, no matter what it seems, is not sad. It's not hopeless. No matter how dark things may seem my light is going to shine. You're going to shine."

It's hard to believe that I'm going to shine. I'm not even able to handle the kids, so Craig has cleared them out of the house. That's why I'm alone to make art today. I put my mountain of dread on my canvas. What I make scares me. It's the truth of how I feel inside. What I feel frightens me. It feels disturbed. I've never made art that's this disturbed before. I add a dark sky to the space around the mountain from my dream. In the darkness I write some words: death, despair, horror, dread and fear. They're scary words but they're honest. I feel so sick inside. In the past I've thought I had reached the bottom, but I was wrong. I can go lower than I have in the past. I just did.

I add a "God's Eye" to the top of the heaping mountain of stones. The God's Eye says, "God knows all." I wonder if God really knows about me right now. I consider all the evidence. I remember all the ways He has been faithful to me. I see that all the evidence points to Him. It all adds up to a God that I can hang my hope on. I add the words "Hope Remains" to my mountain of death and horror. It matters that at my very bottom hope still remains because my hope is slipping. Without hope, my life is purposeless. I have nothing of value to give anyone. I'm so confused. I don't understand my life or my situation. I write a hopeless letter to the only person who has any hope to offer me. He's my only reason that "Hope Remains."

Dear Jesus,

My life amounts to nothing. My hope barely remains. I don't understand You. Why
have You let me reach this terrible place?
**(I have good reasons for the way things
happen. Everything will be used for
My good purposes in the end. Let that
be your hope that remains.)** Jesus, let
these words be true. Let this really be You.
**(I have so much for you. You will come
into the fullness that I have just for you.)**
I'm afraid of failing. I'm afraid of failing You.
**(You can't fail with Me, Alisa. Imagine
your story. Your life lived is the truth
about the battle. You show the world
that the battle can be won. You will be
living proof that the battle is won in Me.)**
It's hard to believe. **(You will see that it's
true. I will make it so.)**

All my hope, that remains, remains in You,
Alisa

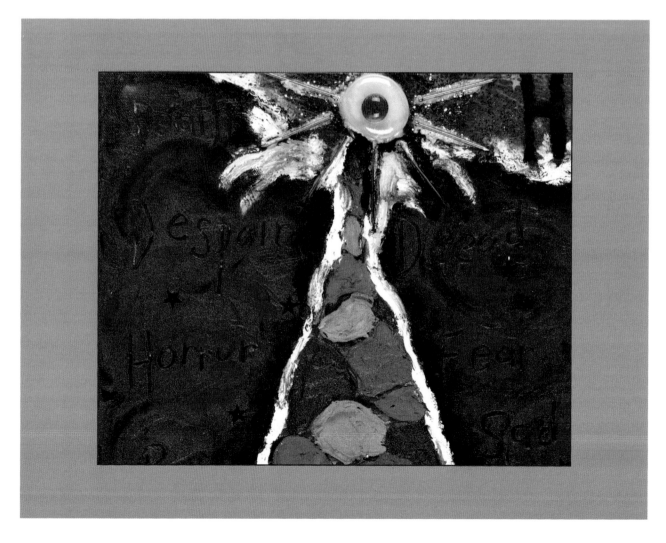

Burning Anger, Age 38

I ask New Therapist for a referral for a better psychiatrist. Better Psychiatrist puts me on a bunch of new drugs. The drugs suck. I feel like my head is stuffed with cotton. I have no desire. I try to write in my journal. It's an enormous effort to locate a pen to put to paper. I tell Jesus how crappy I feel with the hopes that He can revive me.

Dear Jesus,

I'm so tired. I'm zombie tired. Is this part of Your answer? **(For now, it is.)** Where did You go? Where have I gone? I'm a shell of who I was. **(Relax, Alisa. Give your body a chance to adjust. Don't jump to conclusions. And don't ever believe I've left your side.)** Blah. I can barely move the pen across the page. I've lost the desire to connect with You. I'm writing with the hope of getting just a glimmer of what I once had with You. Is there a glimmer? Where are You, Jesus? You feel so far away. I'm so sad. I'm gone. You're gone. **(I am not gone and neither are you. You have to trust Me. You have to give it all time, Alisa. Everything will come together in time.)**

Yours in the fog,
Alisa

The deadness I feel doesn't cut through the anxiety. My gut is wrenching, my muscles are tense and I'm highly irritated. I'm right at the edge and I'm doing the best I can to hide it. I've asked Craig to keep the kids away from me because I'm so anxious and exhausted. It's becoming very difficult to hide the truth from them. I feel so unhinged I could scream, throw things or lose it on my kids. I don't do these things because I'm not nuts just yet. The way some people are treating me right now makes my blood boil. The condescending people, and the people who think they know what I should do, are the worst. They don't offer the help that it's so obvious I need, and they pity me instead of offering real compassion. I feel even more isolated because of them.

I make a collage about anger. It's about burning anger. It's about rage. I make a hot red fire that engulfs the lives of people who share blood with me. The fire shows how angry I am about the way the world is unfair, how it's unfair to others and how it's unfair to me. What I make shows how I feel. I don't like what I make but it's the truth. I'm really, really angry. My anger reminds me of a schizophrenic man I once watched push his wheelchair past me in the streets of New York City. He yelled obscenities and words that were senseless and frightening. I see that while I've never been Schizophrenic Man, I can relate to how he got to be where he is. I've been close enough to the edge to say that he's not so different from me. I'm pissed by how marginalized we both are.

I've got nothing to be proud of. The small chasm between me and this man is little I can pat myself on the back for. All I have to boast for is some undeserved gift of God's grace. I'm no better than this man and I know it. Today I am Schizophrenic Man.

I fight to broaden the chasm. I want to be-

lieve that I'm different. Somehow it makes me feel safe. I've resented some people for doing a poor job of loving me. They hurt me and I saw that as an excuse to put a chasm between us. I decided I was different than them, because I would never do what they had done to me. The truth is that there's very little difference between how they have loved me and how I have loved them. We all have our ways of loving poorly. If the only people we can love well are those who love us well, we're going to be awfully alone. We'll find we don't even have ourselves for company.

I see how God's way is a paradox. When we close the chasm between ourselves and others we find ourselves right where God wants us. When we put ourselves on equal footing with others we discover truth. We see that while we may not all be in prison, we've all lied and cheated. We accept that while we may not all be crazy, we've all done something simply mad. We know that while we may not hate everyone, we've all dished out our share of hatred. Once we see how much we're like the guy to our left and to our right we find our humility. We find strength to love the "unlovable" and we begin to have patience with ourselves. We embrace what most terrifies us: the truth of how broken we all really are. When we no longer consider ourselves to be anything great we begin to discover greatness. We find that we are no longer afraid. We find ourselves loving just about anyone. That's when I believe God really smiles.

I want to make God smile. That's why I talk to Jesus about my anger with the hopes that He can help me forgive. He got treated unfairly. He was mocked and ridiculed in senseless ways. People proclaimed all kinds of assumptions about Him that were false. He had good reasons to be angry with people, but He gave them grace instead. I want to trade my anger in for some grace. Jesus and I had a conversation about how I can make the trade. It went like this:

Dear sweet Jesus,

It's so hard for me to soften my anger. **(Alisa, you're struggling with your own pride. You're angry that you can't hide your anxiety and your struggles. You try and look perfect, but you fail and you know it. You want to look "healed" in front of everyone so you can look perfect. If you're perfect then you can have control over what people see when they see you. You think you can protect yourself from a sinful world by being perfect, but you can't. I'm your source for negotiating your way through this crazy world with peace. All the perfectionism and control you're grappling for can't save you. Only I can.)** Will it ever go away? **(Do you mean, "Will I ever be perfect?" Don't you think that would be a little dangerous for you? If you were perfect you'd have the opportunity to "have it all together." What would your pride do to you then? What would it do to your relationship with Me?)** Are you saying I can't handle being well? **(I'm saying that you can't handle being God. Look at the truth of what you have done to others and what they have done to you. None of you are innocent.)** What do I do with it all? How do I stop becoming angry when someone hurts me? **(Ac-** cept the label. It will be your constant reminder that you're not perfect. It will keep you humble. Accept that you're in the Diagnostic and Statistical Manual of Mental Disorders. Accept that you are "mentally ill." Relax about how others will use your label to discredit you. Your biggest enemy is pride, not the evil in others. Learn to gracefully accept your own limitations. What I want you to do is become more vulnerable. Let people see your weaknesses and don't worry about how people react to them. Stop hiding. Live more honestly. It's OK to admit that you fail, make mistakes and mess things up. Become comfortable with your imperfections. That's the type of honesty and openness I want you to seek.)** Being that vulnerable is embarrassing and humiliating. It puts me at a disadvantage. I'll get taken advantage of, judged and mistreated. **(That's true. I want you to learn to embrace these disadvantages instead of trying to protect yourself from them. Bring your hurt to Me. I will use it to draw you even closer to Me. Let vulnerability drive you to My feet. I won't make you perfect, but I'll help you be more gentle and peaceful. I'll offer you an even richer life with Me. It will be a life that allows you to experience My love in your weakness and sinfulness. It's called a life of grace, and you've been missing out on it. Would you like some grace, Alisa?)** I would, please. (You will learn to receive My grace, Alisa. Today you will begin.) Thank you. (My pleasure.)

Grateful for Your grace,
Alisa

Who I Really Am, Age 38

I have a dream. I'm an ordinary white horse but I become this beautiful, black creature. It has wings so it can fly. It's unique and wonderful. It's like a beautiful stallion, but it's so much more. It's fantastic. I want to fly like my black winged dream creature can fly.

I add my dream black stallion to my canvas. Good apples pelt my black, winged creature. They're red, delicious apples, not peace-stealing crab apples. The red delicious apples bear the names of the fruits of the Spirit from the book of Galatians. With each "hit" my stallion gets something and lets something go. Hatred is traded for love, fear is given away for peace, and sadness is swapped for joy. I give my black horse wings so it can soar.

I am becoming the beautiful black creature in my dreams. I had been the ordinary white horse until I chose to begin absorbing all the evil that was sent my way. That's when I began transforming. I started to understand who I really was. Now I'm learning to embrace each "hit" and understanding, more and more, that the chasm between me and my offender is small. For the first time I am giving a little of the love I wish to receive.

I want to apologize to the people I have not loved well. I have expected much and given little. Please forgive me. I was much afraid. I was trying to be perfect and I was demanding perfection in return. I'm not perfect. I'm really very messed up. I've tried to hide so much from you. It's OK that you've hurt me. I've hurt you too. I'll do my best to accept the pain you've given me. I want to love you anyway. I want to love you even if the best you can do is push me away. Please know how much I want your heart, and your name, to be safe with me. Even if we're not friends I still love you. Even if you hate me, I'm still your friend.

God gives me an encouragement. He tells me something exciting. "You're going someplace new, Alisa," He says. "You've never traveled this way before, but I will guide you." I add these words to the canvas with the beautiful black stallion with wonderful wings. I consider the blessing in what has happened to me. I see the purpose in the sickness and the suffering. It helped me see what I had become, so that I would have the chance to be something new. For the first time I see how incredibly faithful God is. I see how He will do whatever it takes to make the best of who we are.

Forgive me. It takes time to learn to ride a new horse. I'll fall off many times, especially at first. Sometimes my heart will get a little hard again, and I'll try and pretend that I'm something much more than I really am. Please forgive me. I promise I'm gonna learn how to ride this thing. I'm determined to become who I really am. It may take a while, but one day you'll come to trust that most of the time I can be trusted. I won't fall off so much anymore. You'll begin to see the truth. It's the truth that lies deep down within me. It's the truth that I really do wish to love you dearly.

I'm learning to ride my new horse. That's why I do things differently today. I even share differently. I don't struggle to hide the truth as much anymore. It's OK if some people think I'm a little loony. I try to say "I'm sorry" honestly and I do my best to love the people who think the worst of me. I do my best to share my whole story without trying to make it look perfect, or pretty, so people will think better of me. It's a brand new way to share and it feels strangely good. It's especially good, when my story is life for someone else. When my life is someone's lifeline, I know that I really am learning to fly.

Accepting

Out from the Darkness, Age 38

My mother-in-law made me this fantastic coat. It's full of colors and patterns and it's quite unique and very thoughtful. It's a one-of-a-kind creation just for me. It's awesome.

The biblical Joseph got a special coat from his father. Much like mine, it was made especially for him. It was a reminder that God had a special future for him. The coat spoke of his potential before he stepped into it. His brothers ripped his jacket from him, and did their best to strip him of all he was to become, but they couldn't stop God from fulfilling all that He had promised and planned. They tried to destroy Joseph's inheritance but actually helped fulfill it. God used the brothers' efforts to destroy Joseph in order to bring him into the fullness of everything He meant for him to become. It took time but eventually Joseph became all the things his coat promised he would be.

I don't know if my mother-in-law realizes it, but the coat she made me speaks. It speaks of what I am to be: a unique, awesome, one of a kind creation. When I wear it God whispers to me. He says, "I have special plans for you. Just be who you are. Walk with Me in confidence. You will step into all I've promised you."

I don't feel comfortable in my coat yet. It needs to be broken in. The wearings and washings will make it soft and pliable. Attempts have already been made to strip it from me before I'm comfortable in it. I've been teased for wearing it. The coat felt awkward and wrong on me as I was teased. I kept on wearing it, though. I knew that one day I'd put it on and it would feel just right. No one will have a chance of teasing it off of me when that day comes. I'll understand all the things my coat calls me to be, and I'll see that I am stepping into its promises. No one, and nothing, can stop that day from arriving. God will be sure of that.

I have a dream about my Joseph coat. In the dream some words are spoken to me: to be shut forever. The words are encouraging words. They make me feel like there might actually be a way to shut the door on the bad things in my life. In my dream I see myself emerging from a dark, underground crypt that has stairs and a door leading to brilliant light on the outside. The walls of the tomb are thick, dank and heavy. When I open the door to the light the door moans and creaks. I have to push hard, and lean in with all my body weight, to find my way out to the light on the other side. When I step out from the darkness I notice that I've been wearing my colorful coat all along; it's just been too dark for me to know it. My eyes squint in the light. They've been in the dark for so long it takes a while for them to adjust. I step out fully into the freedom of the open air around me. I raise my hands to God and celebrate my escape from below. I live in the light now. Angels soar around me singing, "To be shut forever. What has been is finished. Come dance in the light, Alisa. Your days of darkness have ended. Come celebrate. Come celebrate the light." As I hear the angels' words I notice that my coat of many colors, for the very first time, fits just right.

I know my dream is a promise. Against the reality of what seems to be stands the promise of my dream. One day I will step out of the place I now find myself and into a new place that is full of wonder and joy. I will step into the place that God meant for me all along.

I think about my dream on the way to the doctor's office. He's a new doctor so I pray that he will have a new piece that will help me. "What's wrong?" I ask the new doctor. "Please tell me what's really wrong with me." He gives me the answer that most frightens me. He wants me to take bipolar meds and I'm terrified and confused. I say, "I've never had a manic episode. I've never been really depressed. How am I bipolar?" New Doctor says, "I believe this medicine will help you sleep." I explain how my mom's meds gave her a movement disorder. I tell New Doctor that I'm afraid I'll end up like her. New Doctor says he doesn't think that will happen to me. He's kind, and sweet, and he gives a damn. I decide to accept his answer because it makes some sense. I figure that I might not be exactly like my mom but maybe I'm sorta like her. I'm so far at the end of my rope that on the way to the pharmacy I plead with God. I beg Him to let the bipolar meds work. After years of rejecting anything resembling a bipolar diagnosis, I find myself embracing it. An outcome that once seemed like the end now promises the hope of a new beginning.

I'm afraid of the medication. The possibility it could cause an irreversible movement disorder, or ignite a manic episode, does exist. God asks me if I trust Him. I tell Him that I'm done bargaining with Him. I tell Him that I no longer expect Him to be my magic genie who will make my life on earth like life in Heaven. My prayer is simple. "Lord, if I go crazy please don't leave me. If my body tremors until the day I die please be with me. I accept whatever is necessary for Your will to be done in my life. I accept whatever is needed for Your will to be done through me for others. Your will, Lord, not mine be done." I pray that His will, while strange, hard and sometimes very difficult to understand, will be enough for me.

I surrender. Inside myself I say, "God could need me in the loony bin. If He sends me there I will go. Maybe I'll get a movement disorder, but I understand something new. Some people with movement disorders are dying inside. They need someone just like them to reach out and understand. Maybe that someone needs to be me. Lord, give me courage to become who I need to be. I want my coat to fit just right."

I walk around making friends with my deepest fears. It's not as horrible as I thought it would be. Facing my demons opens dank, heavy doors that lead to the light. I start my new drug cocktail. It's hard at first. My body needs to adjust. I hang on to the promise of my dream. I imagine myself climbing the stairs from the depths and into the freedom. As I advance, I become less like that white horse and more like my winged, black, dream stallion. I imagine that I'm going someplace new. It's someplace I've never been before. When I get there I'll be wearing my coat of many colors, and I'll raise my hands towards Heaven to thank my God for His incredible faithfulness to me.

I tell Jesus about my deepest fears, regrets, confusion, sadness, humiliation and frustration and I do my best to surrender it all. I don't expect a "magic genie" answer. I just talk to Him because I know He'll listen and answer me in His way. More and more, His way is becoming enough for me. I tell Him everything with just a quiet place, a black pen and my journal.

Dear sweet Jesus,

I surrender. I plan to do whatever New Doctor recommends. I'm willing to say, "I could be manic depressive." I'm willing to say it, but I'm very afraid. This is my biggest fear and I have to face it. I'm gonna face it head-on. Protect me, please. Protect me from the things that are not Your will. I'll take the pain, the loss and the humiliation. I'll accept it all. Please just keep me where You want me to be. Please let me hear Your voice. Let the doctor hear Your voice. Give us Your solution. I'll accept a "broken world" solution if I have the assurance that You'll keep me safely in Your will. Please put me in the shadow of Your wings. **(The truth will set you free, Alisa. How about a more humble, broken, honest, fragile Alisa? How about an Alisa who understands the comfort of the promise of My love in a world that gives no promises?)** I'm so afraid. Afraid of what I've done to the kids. I'm afraid, especially, of what I've done to Emily. I'm afraid of the subtle ways I've given this "sickness" space to take root in her. I've tried to avoid passing this on, but I'm afraid I've failed at that. I'm afraid I'll get worse. I'm scared of what will happen when I get worse. I'm afraid of what people will say about me. I'm afraid of the ways I'll be discredited, spoken about behind my back and dismissed. I fear living a life marred by this "sick" thing that's after me. I don't get the Bible anymore. I don't get You. Is there any hope for a better future for me? What about my kids? How is what's happening to me any different than what happened to my mom? **(You believe in Me. That's what is different. No matter what happens you are never alone. I am your joy and your hope. I will surround you with people who will embrace you and respect you in your brokenness. They won't want you perfect. They'll like you just as you are. They'll love you just like I do.)** I'm sad today. **(I know, but that will change. Tomorrow is a new day. It's a day of hope. You will be filled with a new hope for the future. It will be a hope centered in Me, not in what is going to happen. That's where your peace will be found: in Me. You will begin to gain the peace that only I can give.)** Really? **(Really.)**

My hope still remains in You,
Alisa

I'm surrendering. That's why I'm accepting my greatest fears. It's how I'm discovering that those fears don't define me. I meet with New Doctor again. I tell him the bipolar meds are working. We discuss my official diagnosis. It's not what I thought it was. I've been diagnosed with the same diagnosis I started out with two decades ago: anxiety. Nothing has changed. Even my label is still the same.

I take meds that help people who are bipolar. They help me. My new meds help me sleep so now I'm well. I redefine myself. My name is Alisa Clark and I'm not going to the loony bin. My name is Alisa Clark and I'm not going crazy. My name is Alisa Clark and I won't have a movement disorder. My name is Alisa Clark and there is an answer that will make me well. It's the best end result that I could have hoped for. I don't care about what meds I take or what my label is. I don't care what people think about me. What I do care about is being well and I am well. There's nothing for me to be afraid of anymore.

For a while, I thought that what I had feared all my life had come to be. I thought "it" had got me. After a lifetime of running from "it," the Bipolar Beast had gotten me. That's what I thought, anyway. Believing "it" had gotten me ended up being a good thing. Facing the Bipolar Beast dismantled the power it had over me. I walked around for a few weeks as the person I always feared I would become: a person with bipolar disorder. I did OK as a bipolar person. My life didn't end. Ironically, it began. The Beast didn't own me anymore.

I've got to pause and celebrate the miracle that has been realized in my life. I have waited so long to be well. I AM WELL! I can sleep. I no longer sleep on a mat on the floor. Today I sleep in a bed next to Craig. I wake up when the alarm goes off. My head doesn't hurt anymore and I don't feel like it's stuffed with cotton. I still have my joy, my personality and my passions. A little up and down is still a part of me, but I can now make the most of it. I'm ready to do something really amazing with this new life I've been given. bipolar or not, I'm not afraid.

Jesus came on His white horse and took away my unbearable pain. It's why I can now pray with enthusiasm instead of desperation. It's like I'm a brand-new person with a brand-new list of desires. I can pray for things that I've never been able to dream of before. Today, when I pray, I feel like a kid at the candy store. I get to ask for whatever I want and wait patiently, instead of desperately, to get it. I ask Jesus to teach me how to love, and I expect Him to answer. It's a new prayer that's not desperate and pleading. It's hopeful. Today, nothing seems impossible.

I just might do the impossible. The Spectrum is a gift that makes it easy for me to do things others might consider impossible. I'll be honest. I believe I am in The Spectrum. I know that I'm a little nutty, but I like that. It's true that I go up and down a little bit, but I have flavor. I like these things about me. I'm in The Spectrum and it is an awesome place to be in. It allows me creativity, enthusiasm and a beautiful way of seeing the world. I like the way I can get really excited about things. I see beauty where other people miss it. I can easily feel what other people feel, I have a great love for people and I am a person who is really passionate. I am all of these things because they are the blessings of The Spectrum and the blessings of being who I am. I'm not scared of The Spectrum anymore. I'm not afraid to be me. Today I embrace it all.

Not everyone is comfortable with who I am. They can't embrace the new me. It's best to not try and hope they'll be able to see how I'm something new. It's best just to let them be and love them as best as I can. I know that people are just afraid like I once was. I'm not willing to live afraid anymore. Instead, I'm going to live boldly. I'm not hiding what's happened to me to protect my pride. I'm not shrinking back when people accuse me and feel threatened. I want to be a person who is willing to live life emotionally exposed. It hurts when I'm not loved well, but that's not going to stop me from loving back. I'll be trying to love even when it causes me pain. I don't care if that leaves me vulnerable. I'm still going to try and give the grace I've so desperately needed.

Of all the people I have ever known, Craig has offered me the most grace. He doesn't judge me. Craig encourages me and sees me as capable of more than I realize. He knows everything about me, all the mistakes I've made and the bad things that I've done. He still loves me. If I had a nervous breakdown he wouldn't make me feel small. He'd hug me and tell me I was OK. Craig doesn't ignite my deeper fears. Instead he soothes and heals them. When life pushes me down he helps me see that I can push back. He brings me tastes of how God loves me. I am always safe in his arms. That's grace.

Jesus gave grace. Jesus never stopped loving the people who missed who He was and what He was all about. He protected those who murdered Him. He went so far as to make a way to Heaven for his executioners. He celebrated with people who were miles from perfect. He celebrated with tax collectors, law breakers, adulterous women and other evildoers like me. He sacrificed for people who couldn't even

sacrifice a night's sleep before His crucifixion. He loved without expecting anything in return. He loved those who hated Him, gave Him nothing and gave Him very little.

I love who I am today. It's the miracle of unconditional love for others that I'm now after. I don't want to feel squashed and angered by the fingers that accuse and belittle me. Instead, I want to be secure in how Jesus sees me. I want to talk to Jesus and ask Him how I can learn to love others. I want to ask Him how I can better see how He loves me. I have a way to ask Him these things, so I ask:

Hello, Jesus,

How did you do it? How did you love all those people who mocked You and hurt You? **(I didn't place My trust in people. My trust was in My Father in Heaven.)** How is it that You didn't get wounded? **(I felt all the pain you feel when someone hurts you. I loved them anyway. I didn't expect people to be perfect. I didn't expect that they wouldn't hurt Me. I just loved them. Do you think you could learn to love like that?)** I will have to trust that you will help me. It's so hard for me to love the hurting people who hurt me. **(If you want peace, Alisa, you will have to empty yourself of the need to have others be what you trust in. You will also have to accept the emptiness that comes with knowing that I am the only thing you can trust. Do you think it was easy to love on that cross?)** No way. **(It won't be easy for you to love those who persecute you either.)** Love like that seems so impossible. **(You must** work to relinquish your pride and place your trust in Me. As you open yourself to Me in spite of the pain, sin and unfairness of this world you will learn to "let go." People, like you, are clinging to the hope that the world has something to offer their deepest needs. I am their deepest need. Do you see that I am your deepest need, Alisa?) Right now I do, but I forget and get caught up in trying to get my needs met elsewhere. Maybe, deep down inside, I just don't want You enough? (Your desire for relationship with Me is insatiable. That's why your deepest needs won't get met in the world, Alisa: not in your family, in your kids, or even in your own husband. When you stop expecting your needs to be met on this earth, you will love freely. Meanwhile, you and I will dance this bittersweet dance: you choosing to move away from Me empty, and Me drawing you back full. There is pain in the dance. It's the pain of knowing you can't have your deepest needs fully met on this earth mixed with the sweetness of My love for you. Are you willing to dance with Me, Alisa?) I deeply desire to. (I will dance with you. You will dance with your Father who loves you perfectly. I will let you move away and feel the emptiness apart from Me until the force of your desire drives you back to Me.) I'm afraid of how much it will hurt when people don't love me back. (You can't find an answer to your emptiness in this world. You must bring your fear and emptiness to My feet. Then I can bring you peace and make you full. I will also use you to help others find fullness. I will help you as you journey and I will bring you closer and closer to the day when you will love perfectly and your peace will be complete. All of it will be done in Me.) I look forward to that day. (I do, as well.)

Secure in Your love,
Alisa

There's so much to live for. I have blessings and I have a chance at enjoying them. I sleep at night with the rest of the world. I feel fantastic. I'm not just a person who feels good, though. I'm a person who's got a shot at cashing in her anger and bitterness for some love. I've got a shot at loving more every day. I'll do my best to give back something different than what others have given me. I'm going to do my best to give them something good like love, grace or patience. I believe Jesus is going to help me give others these good things. He told me He would and I trust Him.

I trust Him. Today, that's the story I have to share. It's not a story of miraculous healing, a perfect ending or a quick-fix solution. It's the story of an up and down life walked alongside a God who can be trusted. Some people aren't ready to hear my story. They aren't ready to face the realities of living in this broken world because they haven't been broken yet. I've been broken. That's why I have a broken story to share. The people who are ready to hear my story often listen and respond. They give me the comfort of the realities of their own broken life and how it has also been touched by God. Sharing like this is one of the greatest encouragements this life has to offer. With God, every broken life is a powerful story to be shared.

In the Doghouse, Age 38

When I was about eight years old we had a little wooden doghouse that hung from the side of our stove with magnets. Each of us had a dog tag, with our name on it, that could be hung inside the doghouse. It was supposed to be all in fun when we wound up "in the doghouse." It wasn't fun for me, especially, if I wound up "in the doghouse" undeservedly. That would send me reeling. It still sends me reeling.

I think the doghouse sends me reeling because of a voice I have. It's not the God voice. It's a different voice that points out everything I do wrong. It's a voice that makes me feel guilty about every move and breath I take. The Guilt Voice judges me, and gives a guilty verdict, even when I don't really know what I'm guilty of. The Guilt Voice tells me that I deserve to be in the doghouse. The God Voice tells me something different. The God Voice tells me that "guilty" is not what I am. The two voices compete with each other inside my head. I want to hear the God Voice, and silence the Guilt Voice, so I can hear the truth. I have no problem admitting that I'm guilty if I'm sure I am. I want to apologize for the things I've done that aren't good, but I don't want to spend all my time just feeling guilty without knowing what I've done or what I need to change.

There's a place that I can go where the God Voice will speak loudly and clearly and the Guilt Voice is silenced. That place is in my journal. I go to that place because I need it very badly. I can't possibly be as guilty as the Guilt Voice says I am. It's impossible that I should be in the doghouse all the time. The God Voice will tell me the truth about what is possible. I want to hear what the God Voice has to say, so I write.

Dear God,

(Isn't it time you started believing that you are not being judged by Me? I don't want you to spend your life thinking that I want you to be perfect. I want you to spend your life knowing that you are loved by Me.) I need your help. I am responsible for the things I do wrong and I just keep doing them. **(That's not what I see. I see My child and she is more beautiful to Me every moment.)** I don't see myself changing. I'm just the same sinner I was yesterday. I'm not any different. I must be doing something wrong. I feel like I'm doing something very wrong. **(I have made your life a miracle, Alisa. I will give you eyes to see the truth. The Guilt Voice is lying, Alisa. Every day you radiate My love. Each day you radiate just a little more of Me than you did the day before.)** I've been so impatient with Zachy. I feel so guilty about how I'm doing as his mother. **(It's true that you've been impatient. You are not a perfect mother. Some days your heart is much divided and that causes you to fall short. Remember that a divided heart is my business. The Guilt Voice wants you to believe that you have power over your divided heart. You don't. Feeling guilty doesn't change your heart. Feeling guilty keeps you trapped in believing that you have the power to change yourself. What you need to feel is My grace and forgiveness. That's the best way you can give Me good space to work on your heart.)** Some days it's so hard to feel good about myself. When I'm anxious, and feeling overwhelmed, I feel terrible inside. That's when I really feel like I've done something wrong. **(Some of the things your body experiences are beyond your control. There is no simple answer to what happens inside of you. Darkness and light exist within your heart. Your body is broken and it lives within a broken world. Each broken piece is Mine to redeem. You can't redeem it on your own and the Guilt Voice just interferes with what I'm trying to do inside of you. You need to talk to Me when the Guilt Voice starts talking to you. That's how you'll shut it up and begin to know the truth. Then you'll have real repentance. You won't feel condemnation. Instead, you'll feel My just, gentle and fair correction.)** I can't shake the feeling of condemnation. It follows me everywhere. **(Stop and feel that feeling. What is that? Where is that feeling really coming from?)** I must have done something wrong. People are angry with me. **(Do you really believe that you cause people's anger? Are you really responsible for what other people feel?)** On some level, I think I am. I'm always sinning on some level. **(If you spend your life dissecting every breath and move you make you won't live a life of freedom. Instead, you'll live a life as a slave to perfectionism. How about trusting that I will bring you My gentle correction when it is needed?)** My mind keeps replaying the words of the Guilt Voice. I recall the things I've felt, done and said. They play themselves over and over again in my mind. I can't get out of the cycle. **(The Cycle drowns out my voice, Alisa. Shut it down. Shut down that Guilt Voice and let your God Voice take over.)** I must be guilty of something. It's not possible that I'm not. **(Stop trying to figure out what you're doing wrong. Search for the light within you. Look for My goodness, and My Spirit, and let it take over. Make these voices become the tape that plays itself over and over again in your mind. You're looking for the wrong stuff, Alisa. You're looking for proof that you're really bad and you won't find it.)** I'm going to do my best to silence that Guilt Voice. I'm going to need Your help. I can't do it on my own. **(I'm here to help you, Alisa. You will find the courage to hear My voice. I won't let you live your life in the doghouse.)** Thank you. **(You're welcome.)**

Trusting in Your voice,
Alisa

When it's all said and done what I want to prefer most is people. I want to learn to keep comfortable company with all people including the people who put me in the doghouse. My blaming person could also be a loving person. I could discover that they are full of generosity. I might end up in the doghouse once in a while, but I might discover that a person of great integrity put me in there. I don't want to define people using bits and pieces of who they are. I don't want to define others by their lowest moments. I need a new way of defining them. That's why I need to silence the Guilt Voice and hear God's instead. God is my only chance at redefining myself and others. His voice is what I need.

I make a doghouse on my canvas. I add

myself to it. I'm cringing and shrinking back. I ask, "Why am I in here?" Outside the doghouse is a cherry tree with big, juicy, wonderful cherries. I go back to when I was a little girl picking cherries while standing on a ladder my dad is securely holding. I know what to expect from him. He's someone I can count on. I know he won't let me fall. I know he'll always stand for what is good, right and true.

I need to make peace with the doghouse. My dad's honesty is rare. Some people will always put me in the doghouse and I can't control that. Everyone can't offer me fairness and truth. I want to live at peace with them anyway.

I want to believe the truth about myself and others. Right now that's really hard because I'm in the doghouse. I've been put there, and I'm pretty sure I don't deserve to be there. The people who put me in the doghouse think that's where I belong. They don't experience guilt like I do. In fact, I don't know that they experience guilt much at all. Instead, they just react. Nothing I say makes a difference. They just can't imagine that they've done anything wrong because they live guilt free. If they have bad feelings while I'm in the room they decide it must be my fault. The way I see my responsibility is the direct opposite of how they see theirs. I see myself as guilty for everything. They think they're guilty of nothing.

I don't think I would care so much about what other people thought if part of me wasn't so busy listening to the Guilt Voice. In fact, if I believed God's Voice, and silenced the Guilt Voice, I wouldn't be so mad about being in the doghouse. I think I'd even be able to love the people who put me there. The reason why I'm so mad at them is not all their fault. I'm angry because I feel guilty, so I receive their guilt. Extra guilt makes the condemnations stick. I'm sick of all the guilt. It pisses me off. My guilt isn't their responsibility. They're not the only ones who are messed up. I've got a big problem. It's guilt.

I let people know about my struggles with guilt. I tell them about the doghouse, and how it makes me feel, too. These are realities in my life right now and I do my best to be honest about them with others. If I share a neat, clean and tidy story of a life of pure holiness and perfection I offer nothing but a lie. No one needs a story that I can't live up to and they can't live up to either. People need my real story: an imperfect journey of an imperfect person trying her best to be something more. Hopefully, people will see the encouragement and hope my story has to give. That's the hope that we are never alone. It's the encouragement of knowing that with God our lives can mean something more. God is always with us in the ups, downs and in-betweens. We find him in the ordinary, broken places. That's the truth of our lives. That's everyone's story to share.

Dancing in the Doghouse, Age 38

I'm tired of the guilt, anger and condemnation. I want to dance in the doghouse. It takes courage to dance in the doghouse. You can't do it if you're scared and you let other people's woundedness wound you. You have to have the courage to absorb what hurts and return it with gentleness and compassion. You have to have the courage to give the opposite of what you have received.

Some don't agree with how I've chosen to make sense of my life. Some people may not agree with my conclusions. If they know me they likely have their own conclusions. They are not me so they will see things differently. Some people might disregard my feelings or find them confusing or wrong. They don't live inside my mind and my heart. They can't possibly understand. It's my life. I get to remember it in the ways I choose. I get to make sense out of it in the ways it makes sense for me. I get to make my own conclusions and decide how I feel. They're my crocuses in a glass and my purple irises. They're my dreams and my experiences. It's my relationship with people. It's my relationship with God. I get to write the script. I make no apologies for what is found on these pages.

I'm not ashamed of who I am or how I have chosen to live, or think or believe. I'm not sorry for the way I see my life. I'm not sorry for what things mean to me. I'm going to dance in the doghouse even if you won't dance with me. I'm going to remember the beauty and let the rest go.

I'm in the center of a collage. I'm proudly wearing my fantastic coat. My hands are raised in the air and my hair hangs loosely behind me. My skirt flows down to my ankles. My feet are bare. Everything about me is free. I enter the doghouse with reckless abandon and praise. Across the front of the doghouse is the word "courage." It says "courage" because I'm no longer afraid of who I am, and I'm no longer afraid of what others will see.

I see others who are angry and hurt. I see sick people. I see people in pain. I see lonely people and people who are out of hope. I see their chains because they were once mine. (Sometimes they still are mine.) They're on their journey, too. I leave them to be where they are. I pray for them and love them as best I can. They might not like who I am. That's OK. I'm still gonna love them, and I'm still gonna dance in the doghouse.

Will you dance with me? Will you dance with me in the doghouse? People will notice that we're dancing in there. Our lives will tell a new story of forgiveness, patience and love. Others will want to know how we can do it. They'll want to know why were not angry when anger is justified. They'll want to know why we patiently love impatient people. Our way of dancing will draw attention to the new way we have chosen to live. People will want to know our secret. That's why they will ask for our story. Then we can offer it and encourage others to dance with us too.

Connected, Age 38

Suffering is a paradox. You'd think it's a curse but it's really a blessing. In it you discover how much you need God. You thank God for your suffering. You see how it helped you find Him. You see that God is the one thing you've really wanted all along. You join hands and celebrate your discovery with the ordinary, everyday people like me. We're all people who need God.

If life has always left you satisfied you can't celebrate with me yet. You just haven't had a chance to ache for Him. You have no idea how incredible God is. Don't worry. He'll give you a chance to understand the paradox. He's faithful to do it for us all.

I'm not satisfied yet. No way. There's so much more to ache for. I ache for peace, love, joy, gentleness and compassion. I ache to get even closer to what God intended for me to be. I ache for so much

more than just no pain. I'm just starting to be what I hope to be. I tell Jesus what I ache for. I tell Him of what I hope to be. I tell Jesus because He knows how hard it is to love in this crazy world. I tell Jesus because I know that He will help me.

Dear sweet Jesus,

I ache to be a person who's not angry, hurt and full of guilt. I ache for peace, joy, gentleness and compassion. This is a crazy world. I'm surrounded by craziness. How did You do it? How did You love in this crazy world? **(Sin is grasping for people's souls, Alisa. The devil tries to make people believe that they need to be perfect to deserve to be loved. Craziness is the result of living in a world of people who are trying to be perfect. Some of these people are like you; they're full of guilt and they're trying so hard to do ev-**

erything right. Others feel so much guilt that they can't even face it. They've forgotten the truth that they're not perfect. That's why they are people who aren't safe. I walked the world loving people but I didn't love them all in the same way. I didn't pretend that Judas was a safe person. I loved him, but I knew I couldn't pretend that he was able to love me well. I loved in this crazy world because I trusted My Father. I trusted His love for Me and I trusted His voice. He kept My heart safe in an unsafe world.) I let people get too close to me. I do it again and again. I grovel for the affections of people who aren't safe. Then I'm surprised when they hurt me. **(You can love them without giving them your heart. Freedom from codependency starts with learning to put space between yourself and the people around you. Some people can be closer to you than others. You need to listen to Me when I tell you what kind of space is needed in your relationships. This is how you won't get sucked into the crazy worlds other people live in. It's also how you will be able to love people who are "living crazy" in this crazy world.)** I worry that I'm wrong about what I see in people. I keep telling myself that I'm wrong about what I see. I keep telling myself that I must be the one who is wrong. **(I have given you eyes that can see. See the truth and love people as they are. Don't try to make people be something that they cannot be. That's when they become hard for you to love.)** I have so much resentment for the people who have failed me. I'm disappointed in myself, too, for the ways I have failed them. **(I'm really proud of you.**

This is the hard work of learning to love and you are willing to do it. There are differences in you and they're good differences. You're more loving, less rigid, more honest, less manipulative and stronger in Me. It is happening to you, Alisa. The change that only I can make is happening in you. Even self-control is peeking in.) I'm angry. **(That's honest and human.)** I'm unloving. **(That's honest and human, too.)** Help me love the "crazy people" in my life. **(I will reveal the truth of their lives to you. I will show you their struggles so that you can help them heal. You will begin to have compassion for others because of what you see. You will see the vainness of your resentment. You will see how you can love them in the madness. You will see that they are not that much different than you. Just like you, they are people who struggle to hear My voice. Just like you, they are people who, deep down within themselves, ache for a life with Me. Just like you, they struggle with sin and struggle desperately for a life without it. All the people around you, the ones you love and the ones you hate, are just like you.)** Is that why I can't love them until I learn to love myself? **(Exactly.)**

In love with You,
Alisa

I believe what Jesus said. He told me we're not all that different. One Sunday morning my pastor had us play the "I've Never, BUT _____" game. This game reminded me of the ways we're not all that different. If you're human you can play this game. You just put yourself in someone else's shoes to play it. If you ever spanked your kid too hard you could play the game by seeing inside the heart and mind of the child abuser. You'd play the game by saying, "I've never abused a child, BUT I have lost my temper and hit my kid in anger. I'm not a child abuser but I think I understand how it's possible to become one." The game was meant to humble us. It was meant to make us see the ways we are connected to the people around us. It was meant to make us see that we are connected to the good, bad and ugly of life. It was meant to show us that we hold hands with all of humanity, not just the people we know and like.

My latest collage is of two beautiful angels who are holding hands. They remind me of all the people I'm connected to. I'm not connected just to the people I love and care about. I'm connected to the dangerous, speeding driver who cut me off in traffic, the schizophrenic man in the wheelchair, the doctor who is completely indifferent, the lesbian woman seeking acceptance, the man who forgets his baby in the car on a sweltering day, the cashier who burns with rage because of my two extra express lane items, and the nun who squashes a little kid's finger painting. I'm connected to the psychiatrist who forgets about his patients, the people who make sport of marginalizing others, the people who leave me in the doghouse, a teenager who torments little children, the bipolar woman and the person who has no capacity to engage with guilt. I'm connected to the woman who abandons her child, the man who thinks three rounds of electric shock therapy is really wonderful for his mom, Disgusting Guy who mauls me against my will, the

man with a movement disorder, the person who sleeps while their baby is drowning, the catatonic woman and the institutionalized patient. I hold hands with all of these people. I've never ___ BUT only by the grace of God.

I'm not saying that our anger shouldn't rage at injustice or that the guilty should go unpunished. I believe in justice and fairness and truth. Grace is cheap if it doesn't fight for what is right. I am saying that I don't believe we're all that different. Buried down deep inside all of us is something beautiful that we can find to love. The difference between me and a vicious criminal is tragic. They have completely forgotten the truth: people are worth loving well. I'm angry that the world is not a fair place but I hold hands with its offenders and its marginalized. I do so because I am the marginalized. I am an offender too. And I too forget that all people are worth loving well.

My angels remind me of how much we need God. He's the most important reason why I hold hands with the rest of the human race. He's our chance to really get it right. He's the only chance the World Trade Center Bomber has to realize how horribly he has hurt people. He's the only chance I have to realize the same. The difference is only in degree. The offense is still the same. We all fail to love well.

I've hurt people and I've failed to love them well. I've had a secret. It's a secret that's the antithesis of loving. God knew all about my dirty little secret, but I kept it hidden from everyone else. For a long time I lived in denial, having completely buried what I had done when I was a young girl. Later, the truth surfaced, but I kept trying to convince myself that the years that had passed were enough to wipe the slate clean. In reality, I felt just as dirty as I did when I was 14. Time had not healed my wounds. I finally did get sick of hiding. It's only been a few years since I've come clean.

Four years ago I drove to Jackson, Michigan for a counseling appointment. I brought the whole truth with me and I let it be seen. I spoke the words that laid bare what I had done. "The worst part," I said, "is living with Craig without him knowing the truth. He had a right to know my whole story before he married me and we had children. It's not too late to make things right. It's not too late to let him make the choice that he wants to make. I'm afraid because it's possible that he might not choose me. He might choose to feel deceived, angry and ashamed of me. It's his right to feel that way. I'm ashamed of myself. Why shouldn't he be ashamed of me?"

Coming clean wasn't easy but it was necessary. God told me it was time to be honest. My counselor warned me that things might not go well if I told Craig the truth. "It's possible," he said, "that your husband might not handle this well. Are you sure this is what God is telling you to do?" My answer was an unwavering "yes."

In divorce court, my dirty secret would likely give Craig full custody of the kids. I'd be the one getting the every-other-weekend visitation, if I was lucky. Even if Craig did choose to stay married to me, I ran the chance that he might see me with contempt. Maybe he'd get angry and tell other

people what I had done to get revenge. My chances at pleasing anyone would be obliterated. There were a lot of risks, but I was tired of keeping my secret in the dark where it kept me bound. I was tired of asking God to fix something I needed to fix myself. I was willing to risk my marriage, my kids and my reputation for a chance to live honestly.

I have gone way beyond not loving well. I'm connected to some people whom no one wants to ever be connected to. I'm connected to the type of person who deserves to be spit on, beaten in jail or put in line for execution. I haven't ever bombed the World Trade Center, or committed a serious atrocity, but I once dabbled, for just a moment, in serious evil. I stuck my toe in the black pool, to see what it would feel like, and then pulled it out really fast. Then I took off running in the other direction. After that, I was in horror of what could have been and did my best to forget. I didn't want to ever look back.

Some of my friends and family laugh when I tell them that I had my moment as a serious offender. They see me as sweet and innocent. I am neither. I once did a really terrible thing. I'm not sure why I stopped doing it or why I chose not to take it too far. I've disclosed my misdeed to God, my forgiving husband and two of my gracious therapists. No one else knows what I once did, and nobody else needs to know. What I will let others know is that it was a bad thing with some real potential to hurt others. I would have been jailbird potential if I had gone even one step further. I stopped by the grace of God, not because I was a good person.

On that day that I didn't go that one fateful step further, I learned that I had potential to be very good and very bad. I started begging God to make me good. I hated myself for what I had considered. I wanted to be good so I didn't have to hate myself, not because I wanted to love people. I wanted to be good for the wrong reasons. I wanted to be better than the offenders whom I held hands with. I wanted to put space between me and them, so I didn't have to look at my own reflection. That's when the Guilt Voice sunk its claws in me. I've spent my life trying to pull the claws back out again. I've spent my life running from the truth that I'm very far from perfect.

I used to ask God to make me nice so I could feel superior. I wanted God to cure me of my self-loathing so I could look at myself in the mirror and like what I saw. I begged God to absolve me so I wouldn't have to speak the words that would shed light on my darkness. I didn't want to speak the words, "I am a terrible sinner." I prayed that my life would be perfect and that I would never be sick or in pain. I asked God to take my guilt and shame away. I also prayed for stuff and for things to go my way. I used God. I look back on what I've felt about people, all the ways I've been angry and hated, and everything I've feared, run from and done. As I look back and see who I've been, I ache to be someone new. I have a new prayer. Today, this is how I pray: "Jesus, let me love better today than I did yesterday. Let me let go of the things that stop me from loving well. Send Your angels to encourage me. Send Your Spirit to convict me. Send Yourself to change me. Remind me always that I am connected to others. Let me remember that I hold hands with them. Give me the ability to love them well. Give us the ability to love each other well."

Don't we all ache to be someone new? Secretly, don't we all wish we really knew how to love? Deep down inside, isn't the buried desire the same within all of us? Are we really all that different, or do we all actually have the same fundamental stories to share: stories of people who desire to be something more than they already are? I've done a lousy job of it, but I really want to be living the life of a loving person. That's always been my deepest desire. Every move I've made, every word I've spoken, each canvas I've completed and all the stories I've shared have one common thread. It's the desire to live the life of a loving person. It's the desire to be something more. Today, it's that desire I share. Today, that desire is my story and the story of all of those who share.

Maybe we'd all be better off if we didn't fuel each other's desire to be something more? We might fail miserably. Is it really wise to share? I believe it is. Sharing is the greatest hope and encouragement we have to give to the lives that ache for more. If we don't share, our desires remain silent. Hope is squashed. The power to be something more is lost. Our stories ignite hope, so they must be told. We have to speak, because what we speak is hope. It's hope that it's worth reaching for what we hope to be. We tell our stories so the hope doesn't die. We can live the lives of loving people. It's true that we can be something more.

Have It All, Age 39

I can be something more, but I can't do it on my own. In my own power I am nothing, and I have no love or hope to offer anyone. I must surrender. I have to give up all my ways of trying to do it all my own way. Every fear, expectation and selfish desire must be relinquished to make room for God. Then He can do His work. Then He can begin to make me something more.

I'm going to end with surrender. It's the only ending that makes sense for me. It has been my key to health and freedom. It has been my key to life and love. It has become my key to live life with the ease and delight of being God's child once again. It is my chance for tastes of life without fear. Surrender is giving Jesus my life. I tell Him that He can have it all.

Dear sweet Jesus,

I give it all to You, Lord, and I trust You with it all. I give You my guilt, my perfectionism, my mistakes and failings, my codependency, my anger, my rage, hatred and my desire to be as perfect as You. Take my ways of seeing the world: my righteousness, my self-centeredness and the distance I try to put between myself and others. I give You my kids, my husband, my marriage, my family, my body, my sickness, my healing, my perceptions, my hopes and my dreams. I accept Your truth and Your answers. I take Your plans and Your power. I invite You to change all of me. I surrender. You can have it all.

Take my life,
Alisa

I really began to be free when I told Jesus that He could have it all. That's the day I told Him I would keep on living even if He didn't heal me. I released to Him my whole life, whether I got to be healthy or not. Then I gave Him what I feared. I told Him that I would agree to go anywhere, and I would trust Him there. I told Him that I'd go to the mental institution, and I'd live my life with Parkinson's. I agreed to go where He sent me. I gave over my anxiety; I let God have my worry and my worry about my worry. After that, I gave Him my desire for justice. I decided it was time to stop expecting fairness in exchange for love. I agreed to do my best to love people who wounded me and gave me their anger. I turned over my codependency: my need to control relationships, my manipulative ways to gain acceptance and my striving for power. I gave Him my bitterness with the hopes that I might resent less and give more. I handed Him my battle with the Guilt Voice. I gave Him my children, and that was really hard. I've always fought so hard to protect them. I gave Him my mom and dad. I gave Him my husband. I gave Him my finances. I released my family, my friends, my reputation, my hopes and my dreams.

Don't get me wrong. I'm no expert in surrender. I often try to take back what I've given away. God and I are doing a dance. It's one step forward, two steps back. Three steps forward, ten steps back. Yours, mine, Yours, mine, Yours, mine! The good news is that despite the dance, I've managed to move forward. The good news is that most of us do. It's the dance of life. We're all in it.

I laugh at the phrase, "Life is killing me." It's

kinda like the tongue-in-cheek definition of surrender. As we let go of what we want, we have more life. I look back on the canvas of my life and reflect on the things that have given me life: my childhood, my memories, my parents' backyard, the house I was born in, my mom, my dad, my family, the gazebo with a thousand windows, friends, apple trees, my children, my husband, butterflies, picking cherries with my dad, New York, gardens teeming with life, purple irises, yellow crocuses, deer eating apples, playing with my brother at the seashore, my big sister's magic bag, my oldest brother's never-ending bag of potato chips, miracle trees, butterflies, pumpkins, swirly wrought-iron furniture, dancing donkeys and fairies, Christmas with my family, the way Zachy smells after a bath, my coat of many colors, AJ defending the goal, my paintings and even my angels. I know I can't hold on to any of these things too tightly. Once one of them becomes too important to me I become a slave. When I surrender them I'm free to embrace whatever gifts life hands me that day. That's life. Die to live. It's the only way.

I want life. I want to love. I ache to be something more. I no longer expect anything more from my story than my story has to give. Instead, I give all my expectations away. I surrender them. It's OK that I'm not perfect. It's all right that I don't love as much as I should. I accept that others don't give me the love that I ache for. I surrender what I need, what I want and who I am. Surrender is my key to life and love. It has become the fuel for my story.

It's the ultimate irony; in order to truly enjoy life we have to surrender it. We have to see it's not ours for the keeping. We understand that nothing is ours to keep, anyway, unless we want to die a slave. I'd rather submit it all and live. That's what I'm going to try to do for the rest of my journey. In fact, I've decided what will fill my next canvas. It's going to hold all the stuff I'm going to surrender. It's going to be filled with all the things I'm going to give away. My new canvas is going to resonate with life. It's going to tell everyone my story.

Dear Dee,
I hope my journey will encourage you in yours. Enjoy the journey and then share it!
Love,

Tell Everyone Your Story

Epilogue

I haven't sat at the codependents' table for some time now. I miss going to my support group. Attending it has been trumped by a more important commitment. AJ has discovered a passion for baseball. On Mondays I miss my meeting in order to sit on the sidelines and wait for AJ's next turn at bat. It's a good reason to leave my spot empty for a little while, and I know it's waiting for me. I'm glad to watch AJ play baseball, and I'm glad that I'll get to reclaim my spot when baseball season ends. I miss the courage and encouragement that I get at the table. I miss the opportunities I get to share. I'm eager to return.

Adversity, I expect, has not passed over my Monday night friends in my absence. It certainly has not passed over me. I wonder what lessons my group will teach me when I return? I wonder how the experiences of my passing weeks will encourage them when I go back to share? Our circumstances may be different than they were when we last met, but the biggest challenge we face is unchanging. It's the challenge to surrender every part of our lives. At the table we're all figuring out how to give it all away. We're learning to submit so that we might better live. This is the reality that most connects us. It's not an earth-shattering reality. It's the ordinary, everyday truth of our daily lives: surrendering to God is the key to life.

My spot awaits me. I'm glad it's there. Sharing my journey will always be one of the greatest opportunities of my life. Receiving the journeys of others will always be one of life's greatest gifts to me. I look forward to giving and receiving. I look forward to returning, learning and sharing. I anticipate our lives intersecting. God assures me that we will be encouraged, touched and healed by the common threads of our daily lives. I am certain that our ordinary lives will be touching lives for as long as we are willing to take our spot at the table and share.

God really does incredible things with an ordinary life. I know this is true because of the simple ways the rhythms and realities of the lives of others have been lifesaving for me. I know of few things more incredible than the ways the lives of others have breathed life into my very soul. God is truly the King of the ordinary and the Author of the extraordinary. He uses our ordinary lives to do His greatest work. It is my prayer that He has used mine. It is why I have told my story.

Let God Use Your Story

King of the Ordinary

Your hand in every life~
Your purpose in every moment~
Lord of the extraordinary~
King of the ordinary~
Our awesome God.

Praise Him, Age 39

Made in the USA
Charleston, SC
16 January 2011